The 7 Wisdom Books

An Introduction to the Wisdom Books of the Old Testament and the Apocrypha

Francis Brown

This book is dedicated to my parents.

CONTENTS

1. What are the Wisdom Books?

The wisdom books of the Bible help people cope
with the difficulties of life. These writings give
advice (or instruction) on daily living, discuss the
relationships of people with one another, discuss the
relationships of people with God, discuss such
topics as good and evil, why people suffer, why
there is injustice in the world, and so on. Always
included among the wisdom books are the Book of
Job, Proverbs, and Ecclesiastes. The majority of the
Book of Psalms and the Song of Solomon are not
always considered wisdom literature. (This is due to
differences of opinion on what should be included
under the topic of wisdom.) There are two wisdom
books in the Apocrypha, the Wisdom of Solomon
and Ecclesiasticus. Ecclesiasticus is also called the
Wisdom of Sirach or just Sirach.

1

What are the Septuagint and the Apocrypha?

A Jewish community grew rapidly in Alexandria, Egypt after the conquests of Alexander the Great. Over time, a large part of the Jewish population in Alexandria forgot Hebrew and spoke only Hellenistic Greek. This was a problem for the leaders of the community since it made it difficult to teach Hebrew scripture in the synagogues. In Palestine, Hebrew remained the language of Jewish scripture, but Aramaic replaced it as the common language of everyday living. Aramaic had been the official language of the Persian Empire and had been increasingly used by the Jews since their liberation from Babylon. Though Greek was also spoken in Palestine, particularly in business dealings, Aramaic continued to be used extensively in Palestine even as Geek replaced it in other parts of the former Persian Empire. Aramaic was very similar to ancient Hebrew and made it easy to teach scripture. Aramaic, however, was not spoken in Alexandria. The Jews in Alexandria needed Greek translations of scripture. Tradition has it that 70 (or 72) translators worked on translating Hebrew scripture into Greek during the reign of Ptolemy II Philadelphus, who ruled Egypt from 289-244 B.C. It is not known who these translators were or how long it took, but the end result was the Septuagint, named for the 70 translators of tradition.

The Septuagint eventually included not only older traditional Hebrew scripture but additional writings such as the Wisdom of Solomon and Sirach. There are differences between the Hebrew scriptures and the Greek translations, with some books being a little longer and others being a little shorter. The Book of Job, for instance, is about 400 versus shorter in the Greek than in the Hebrew. These differences are probably due to the difficulty of translating Hebrew into Greek and making it understandable to the reader. Also, from the very beginning, some felt that parts of the Septuagint were just bad translations of the Hebrew. Either way, the Septuagint proved to be very popular with both Jews and non-Jews alike and was extremely important to the early Christian Church.

After the destruction of the Temple in AD 70, there was a move by the rabbis in Palestine to return to the Hebrew version of scriptures and to limit what scriptures were considered most important or canonical. However, the Septuagint remained popular in the Jewish community so around AD 140 a new, stricter Greek translation was introduced among Greek speaking Jews. This new version was not accepted by the majority of Christians who continued to use the older version (or versions).

Throughout this time, it was unclear as to which scripture writings were the most important or the most authentic. In Palestine, the rabbis (who taught scripture in Hebrew) began to form a consensus around 24 books. By AD 200, these books would become the Hebrew Canon. The 24 books of the Hebrew Canon are included in the Old Testament of all Christian Bibles. In Christian Bibles, these 24 books would over time become 39 books as some of the longer books were made into 2 or more smaller books.

As the early Christian Church grew, Latin translations of the Bible began to appear as Latin was the common language of the Roman Empire. These translations differed greatly so Pope Damasus I chose Jerome (Saint Jerome) to translate a new standard Latin Bible. Jerome spent 20 years on this endeavor, finishing around AD 404. The end result was the Latin Vulgate, the main Bible of the Catholic Church for centuries. Many expected Jerome to translate the Greek Septuagint into Latin. Instead, Jerome translated the Hebrew Canon into Latin. He did include other books in the Old Testament, but these he labeled Apocrypha in prefaces to distinguish them from the books translated from the Hebrew Canon. As the Vulgate was copied over time, the distinction of Apocrypha was left out in many copies. Later, the Catholic Church would label the Apocrypha books as Deuterocanonical books, meaning they have the same status as the books from the Hebrew Canon. The books translated from the Hebrew canon are called protocanonical books.

Protestant Christians rejected the notion that the Apocrypha books are of equal importance to the 39 books from the Hebrew Canon. That is why the Protestant Old Testament is 39 books, shorter than other Christian Bibles. Protestants do consider the Apocrypha books to be honored works, just not of canonical status

Orthodox Christians continued to use the Septuagint as the basis for their Old Testament. The number of books in the Orthodox Old Testament varies among Orthodox Churches. However, all

Orthodox Bibles include The Wisdom of Solomon and Sirach.

So, of the seven wisdom books, five are part of the Hebrew Canon and are considered canonical by Protestant, Catholic and Orthodox Christians. Two of the books come from the Septuagint and are also considered canonical by Catholic and Orthodox Christians. What follows is a brief introduction to each book.

2. The Book of Job

There is no book of the Bible more debated than Job. Scholars disagree about when it was written, its proper format, if one or multiple authors wrote it, and what it actually says. We do know that the story of Job is very old, probably dating to around 2000 B.C. The book that we have today was written much later, sometime after 1000 B.C. The Book of Job is the longest ancient Hebrew poem known and is considered a literary masterpiece.

Chapters 1-2: The Prologue

We are introduced to Job who lived in the land of Uz (or the land of Ausistis in the Orthodox Bible). It is generally assumed that Job was a gentile, but he could have lived before Abraham and the creation of the Hebrew nation. Job was a man of great integrity who believed in the one all-powerful God.

One day, unbeknownst to Job, God is meeting with his angels when Satan shows up and the following exchange occurs:

1:7 The LORD said to Satan, "Where have you come from?" Satan answered, "From going back and forth in the earth, and from walking up and down in it."
1:8 The LORD said to Satan, "You have noticed my servant, Job? For there is none like him in all the earth, a blameless and upright man, one who fears God and turns away from evil."
1:9 Satan answered the LORD, "Does Job fear God for nothing?
1:10 Haven't you made a hedge around him, around his house, and around all that he has, on every side? You have blessed the work of his hands, and his substance is increased in the land.
1:11 But put forth your hand now and take away all that he has, and he will curse you to your face."
1:12 The LORD said to Satan, "All right, all that he has is in your power. Only do not harm his person." So Satan went forth from the presence of the LORD.

Satan immediately sets about tormenting Job. He kills his farm animals, his servants and then kills all his sons and daughters. Job's response to this horror is not what Satan expected:

1:20 Job arose, and tore his robe, and shaved his head, and fell down on the ground, and worshiped.

1:21 He said, "Naked I came out of my mother's womb, and naked shall I return. The LORD gave, and the LORD has taken away. Blessed be the name of the LORD."

1:22 In all this, Job did not sin, nor charge God with wrongdoing.

Satan failed to turn Job away from God. There is another meeting of God and his angels and Satan once again shows up. He wants to test Job a second time. This time he wants to take away Job's health. God relents and Satan covers Job with boils from head to foot. Satan thinks that this physical pain combined with his immense grief will turn Job away from God. Job does not turn away. Satan fails a second time.

Three of Jobs friends hear about what has happened and come to console Job. These friends are: Eliphaz the Terminate, Bildad the Shuhite, and Zophar the Naamathite. When they see Job, they are shocked by his grief and "Then they sat upon the ground with him for seven days and seven nights, and none spoke a word to him: for they saw that his grief was very great." (Job 2:13)

Chapters 3-27: The Dialogue

Job and his friends sit for seven days and nights without saying a word. Eliphaz, Bildad, and Zophar are (like Job) gentiles who believe in the one all-powerful God. All four men are unaware of the existence of Satan, the struggle between God and

Satan, and that Job has become a focal point in that struggle.

Job is the first to break the silence with a speech illustrating his despair. He wishes he had never been born. He wishes he was dead (but he never contemplates suicide). He wonders why life is given to those with no hope of happiness.

Eliphaz speaks next. He seems a little annoyed by Job's outburst. He says:

4:2 "If someone ventures to talk with you, will you be upset? But who can withhold himself from speaking?

4:3 Look, you have instructed many, you have strengthened the weak hands.

4:4 Your words have supported him who was falling, you have made firm the weak knees.

4:5 But now trouble comes to you, and you faint. It touches you, and you are disturbed.

4:6 Isn't your piety your confidence? Isn't the integrity of your ways your hope?

4:7 Do you ever recall whoever have perished being innocent? Or when were the upright destroyed?

4:8 According to what I have seen, those who plant iniquity, and sow trouble, reap the same.

4:9 By the breath of God they perish. By the blast of his anger they are consumed."

In Eliphaz's opinion, Job should know better than to complain in the manner that he did. Furthermore, Job must have done something wrong or this trouble wouldn't be happening to him. Eliphaz goes on to advise Job to present his case to God and ask forgiveness for whatever sin caused these calamities and God will rescue him.

Job responds by saying that he has a right to complain because of his great misery. He is not guilty of any great sin. He would like to know why God is doing this to him. He is angry with his friends for accusing him of being responsible for what has happened. Why won't they believe he is innocent?

This first exchange of the dialogue is fairly representative of the entire dialogue. The friends are convinced that Job must have done something wrong. They base this on their view of God and their understanding of how the world works. If you obey God's teachings, you will be rewarded; if you don't, you will be punished. Job actually agrees with this world view and he doesn't understand why God is punishing him (remember, Job doesn't know that it is Satan who is tormenting him). Job always thought he had a good relationship with God but now he feels abandoned. Job never turns away from God, but has God turned away from Job?

There are three rounds of speeches in the dialogue with each friend making a speech in the first two rounds and Job responding to each one. However, in the third round, Eliphaz and Bildad make a speech but Zophar does not. This lack of a third speech combined with the sudden appearance of Elihu later on in chapter 32 have led many to believe that the original work was altered at a later date. If changes were made, they were made in ancient times. We know this because an Aramaic

Targum (Targum means interpretation) of the Book of Job was found among the Dead Sea Scrolls in the caves of Qumran. This Targum is very similar to the version we have today. Either way, the dialogue ends with Job's last response to Bildad.

Chapter 28: The Wisdom Poem

After the dialogue comes the Wisdom Poem. The poem was probably written to be spoken by the narrator, but it may have been assigned to Job. The poem states that even though people have gained much knowledge, it is impossible for any person to find wisdom on their own nor is it possible for anyone to buy wisdom. God alone knows the way to wisdom. The poem ends with "the fear of the Lord, that is wisdom. To depart from evil is understanding." (Job 28:28)

Chapters 29-31: Job's Monologue

Job recounts his former life and his present misery. People who he helped in the past now shun him. Young men make fun of him. He is an object of ridicule and scorn as he sits on an ash heap. Job cries out to God: "What are my sins? Why am I being punished?" Job wants to be heard and defend himself before God.

Chapters 32-37 Elihu's Monologue

Elihu son of Barakel the Buzite, of the clan of Ram, makes his appearance. As already noted, many scholars (but not all) think that this monologue was added later by another author since Elihu is not mentioned anywhere else in the poem. Elihu thinks that Eliphaz, Bildad, and Zophar have failed in their arguments. They have been too easy on Job. In his opinion, Job has committed the sin of arrogance in questioning God.

Chapters 38-41: God Speaks to Job

Job has asked to see God. He needs to know that God has not abandoned him. God appears before Job, shrouding himself in a whirlwind. This is a great gift. Job needed to see God and God answered this need. Job thought God had abandoned him, but God was there all the time.

As already stated, Job and his friends share the same view of how the world works: If you obey God's law, you will be rewarded and if you don't, you will be punished. Job believes he has kept his end of the bargain and that God has let him down. God lets Job know that this view is wrong:

38:1 Then the LORD answered Job out of the whirlwind,

38:2 "Who is this who darkens counsel by words without knowledge?

38:3 Brace yourself like a man, for I will question you, then you answer me.

38:4 Where were you when I laid the foundations of the earth? Declare, if you have understanding.

38:5 Who determined its measures, if you know? Or who stretched the line on it?

38:6 Whereupon were its foundations fastened? Or who laid its cornerstone,

38:7 when the morning stars sang together, and all the sons of God shouted for joy?

38:8 Or who shut up the sea with doors, when it broke forth from the womb,

38:9 when I made clouds its garment, and wrapped it in thick darkness,

38:10 marked out for it my bound, set bars and doors,

38:11 and said, 'Here you may come, but no further. Here your proud waves shall be stayed?'

38:12 Have you commanded the morning in your days, and caused the dawn to know its place;

38:13 that it might take hold of the ends of the earth, and shake the wicked out of it?

38:14 It is changed as clay under the seal, and stands forth as a garment.

38:15 From the wicked, their light is withheld. The high arm is broken.

38:16 Have you entered into the springs of the sea? Or have you walked in the recesses of the deep?

38:17 Have the gates of death been revealed to you? Or have you seen the gates of the shadow of death?

38:18 Have you comprehended the earth in its breadth? Declare, if you know it all.

38:19 What is the way to the dwelling of light? As for darkness, where is its place,

38:20 that you should take it to its bound, that you should discern the paths to its house?

38:21 Surely you know, for you were born then, and the number of your days is great.

38:22 Have you entered the treasuries of the snow, or have you seen the treasures of the hail,

38:23 which I have reserved against the time of trouble, against the day of battle and war?

38:24 By what way is the lightning distributed, or the east wind scattered on the earth?

38:25 Who has cut a channel for the flood water, or the path for the thunderstorm;

38:26 To cause it to rain on land where no man is; on the wilderness, in which there is no man;

38:27 to satisfy the waste and desolate ground, to cause the tender grass to spring forth?

38:28 Does the rain have a father? Or who fathers the drops of dew?

38:29 Out of whose womb came the ice? The gray frost of the sky, who has given birth to it?

38:30 The waters become hard like stone, when the surface of the deep is frozen.

38:31 Can you fasten the chains of the Pleiades, or loosen the cords of Orion?

38:32 Can you lead forth the constellations in their season? Or can you lead the bear with her cubs?

38:33 Do you know the laws of the heavens? Can you establish its dominion over the earth?

38:34 Can you lift up your voice to the clouds, that abundance of waters may cover you?

38:35 Can you send forth lightnings, that they may go? Do they report to you, 'Here we are?'

38:36 Who has put wisdom in the inward parts? Or who has given understanding to the mind?

38:37 Who can number the clouds by wisdom? Or who can pour out the bottles of the sky,

38:38 when the dust runs into a mass, and the clods of earth stick together?

38:39 Can you hunt the prey for the lioness, or satisfy the appetite of the young lions,

38:40 when they crouch in their dens, and lie in wait in the thicket?

38:41 Who provides for the raven his prey, when his young ones cry to God, and wander for lack of food?

39:1 Do you know the time when the mountain goats give birth? Do you watch when the doe bears fawns?

39:2 Can you number the months that they fulfill? Or do you know the time when they give birth?

39:3 They bow themselves, they bring forth their young, they end their labor pains.

39:4 Their young ones become strong. They grow up in the open field. They go forth, and do not return again.

39:5 Who has set the wild donkey free? Or who has loosened the bonds of the swift donkey,

39:6 Whose home I have made the wilderness, and the salt land his dwelling place?

39:7 He scorns the tumult of the city, neither does he hear the shouting of the driver.

39:8 The range of the mountains is his pasture, He searches after every green thing.

39:9 Will the wild ox be content to serve you? Or will he stay by your feeding trough?

39:10 Can you hold the wild ox in the furrow with his harness? Or will he till the valleys after you?

39:11 Will you trust him, because his strength is great? Or will you leave to him your labor?

39:12 Will you have faith in him, that he will bring in your grain, and gather it to your threshing floor?

39:13 The wings of the ostrich wave proudly; but are they the feathers and plumage of love?

39:14 For she leaves her eggs on the earth, warms them in the dust,

39:15 and forgets that the foot may crush them, or that the wild animal may trample them.

39:16 She deals harshly with her young ones, as if they were not hers. Though her labor is in vain, she is without fear,

39:17 because God has deprived her of wisdom, neither has he imparted to her understanding.

39:18 When she lifts up herself on high, she scorns the horse and his rider.

39:19 Have you given the horse might? Have you clothed his neck with a quivering mane?

39:20 Have you made him to leap as a locust? The glory of his snorting is awesome.

39:21 He paws in the valley, and rejoices in his strength. He goes out to meet the armed men.

39:22 He mocks at fear, and is not dismayed, neither does he turn back from the sword.

39:23 The quiver rattles against him, the flashing spear and the javelin.

39:24 He eats up the ground with fierceness and rage, neither does he stand still at the sound of the trumpet.

39:25 As often as the trumpet sounds he snorts, 'Aha!' He smells the battle afar off, the thunder of the captains, and the shouting.

39:26 Is it by your wisdom that the hawk soars, and stretches her wings toward the south?

39:27 Is it at your command that the eagle mounts up, and makes his nest on high?

39:28 On the cliff he dwells, and makes his home, on the point of the cliff, and the stronghold.

39:29 From there he spies out the prey. His eyes see it afar off.

39:30 His young ones also suck up blood. Where the slain are, there he is."

40:1 Moreover, the LORD answered Job,

40:2 "Shall he who argues contend with the Almighty? He who argues with God, let him answer it."

Job's First Response:

40:3 Then Job answered the LORD,

40:4 "Look, I am of small account. What shall I answer you? I lay my hand on my mouth.

40:5 I have spoken once, and I will not answer; Yes, twice, but I will proceed no further."

God Continues Speaking to Job:

40:6 Then the LORD answered Job out of the whirlwind,

40:7 "Now brace yourself like a man. I will question you, and you will answer me.

40:8 Will you even annul my judgment? Will you condemn me, that you may be justified?

40:9 Or do you have an arm like God? Can you thunder with a voice like him?

40:10 Now deck yourself with excellency and dignity. Array yourself with honor and majesty.

40:11 Pour out the fury of your anger. Look at everyone who is proud and bring him low.

40:12 Look at everyone who is proud and humble him. Crush the wicked in their place.

40:13 Hide them in the dust together. Bind their faces in the hidden place.

40:14 Then I will also admit to you that your own right hand can save you.

40:15 See now, Behemoth, which I made as well as you. He eats grass like an ox.

40:16 Look now, his strength is in his thighs. His force is in the muscles of his belly.

40:17 He moves his tail like a cedar. The sinews of his thighs are knit together.

40:18 His bones are like tubes of bronze. His limbs are like bars of iron.

40:19 He is the chief of the ways of God. He who made him gives him his sword.

40:20 Surely the mountains produce food for him, where all the animals of the field play.

40:21 He lies under the lotus trees, in the covert of the reed and the marsh.

40:22 The lotuses cover him with their shade. The willows of the brook surround him.

40:23 Look, if a river overflows, he doesn't tremble. He is confident, though the Jordan swells even to his mouth.

40:24 Shall any take him when he is on the watch, or pierce through his nose with a snare?

41:1 Can you draw out Leviathan with a fishhook, or press down his tongue with a cord?

41:2 Can you put a rope into his nose, or pierce his jaw through with a hook?

41:3 Will he make many petitions to you, or will he speak soft words to you?

41:4 Will he make a covenant with you, that you should take him for a servant forever?

41:5 Will you play with him as with a bird? Or will you bind him for your girls?

41:6 Will traders barter for him? Will they part him among the merchants?

41:7 Can you fill his skin with barbed irons, or his head with fish spears?

41:8 Lay your hand on him. Remember the battle, and do so no more.

41:9 Look, the hope of him is in vain. Won't one be cast down even at the sight of him?

41:10 None is so fierce that he dare stir him up. Who then is he who can stand before me?

41:11 Who has first given to me, that I should repay him? Everything under the heavens is mine.

41:12 I will not keep silence concerning his limbs, nor his mighty strength, nor his goodly frame.

41:13 Who can strip off his outer garment? Who shall come within his jaws?

41:14 Who can open the doors of his face? Around his teeth is terror.

41:15 Strong scales are his pride, shut up together with a close seal.

41:16 One is so near to another, that no air can come between them.

41:17 They are joined one to another. They stick together, so that they can't be pulled apart.

41:18 His sneezing flashes out light. His eyes are like the eyelids of the morning.

41:19 Out of his mouth go burning torches. Sparks of fire leap forth.

41:20 Out of his nostrils a smoke goes, as of a boiling pot over a fire of reeds.

41:21 His breath kindles coals. A flame goes forth from his mouth.

41:22 There is strength in his neck. Terror dances before him.

41:23 The flakes of his flesh are joined together. They are firm on him. They can't be moved.

41:24 His heart is as firm as a stone, yes, firm as the lower millstone.

41:25 When he raises himself up, the mighty are afraid. They retreat before his thrashing.

41:26 If one attacks him with the sword, it can't prevail; nor the spear, the dart, nor the pointed shaft.

41:27 He counts iron as straw; and bronze as rotten wood.

41:28 The arrow can't make him flee. Sling stones are like chaff to him.

41:29 Clubs are counted as stubble. He laughs at the rushing of the javelin.

41:30 His undersides are like sharp potsherds, leaving a trail in the mud like a threshing sledge.

41:31 He makes the deep to boil like a pot. He makes the sea like a pot of ointment.

41:32 He makes a path shine after him. One would think the deep had white hair.

41:33 On earth there is not his equal, that is made without fear.

41:34 He sees everything that is high. He is king over all the sons of pride."

Job's Second Response to God:

42:1 Then Job answered the LORD,

42:2 "I know that you can do all things, and that no purpose of yours can be restrained.

42:3 You asked, 'Who is this who hides counsel without knowledge?' therefore I have uttered that which I did not understand, things too wonderful for me, which I did not know.

42:4 You said, 'Listen, now, and I will speak; I will question you, and you will answer me.'

42:5 I had heard of you by the hearing of the ear, but now my eye sees you.

42:6 Therefore I abhor myself, and repent in dust and ashes."

Job (along with his friends) suffered from what the historian Daniel Boorstin called the "illusion of knowledge." Job is certain that he knows the truth and never questions his own understanding of how the world works. God corrects him. Perhaps Job's view was correct for the Garden of Eden, but people no longer live there, they live in this world. In this world, people (as well as God's other creatures) are not exempt from the rules of nature. This world does not revolve around humans. As in Chapter 38 verse 26, it is going to rain on a piece of land whether people are on it or not. This is a world with many wondrous things. It is also a world with many dangers. The reader (unlike Job and his friends) knows that one of those dangers is Satan.

Job realizes his arrogance and accepts God's instruction. Job's trust in God has been justified. He knows that God will never abandon him.

Chapter 42:7-17 The Conclusion

God now turns his attentions to the three friends:

42:7 It was so, that after the LORD had spoken these words to Job, the LORD said to Eliphaz the Temanite, "My wrath is kindled against you, and against your two friends; for you have not spoken of me the thing that is right, as my servant Job has.

42:8 Now therefore, take to yourselves seven bulls and seven rams, and go to my servant Job, and offer up for yourselves a burnt offering; and my servant Job shall pray for you, for I will accept him, that I not deal with you according to your folly. For you have not spoken of me the thing that is right, as my servant Job has."

42:9 So Eliphaz the Terminate and Bildad the Shuhite and Zophar the Naamathite went, and did what the LORD commanded them, and the LORD accepted Job.

23

42:10 The LORD turned the captivity of Job, when he prayed for his friends. The LORD gave Job twice as much as he had before.

42:11 Then came there to him all his brothers, and all his sisters, and all those who had been of his acquaintance before, and ate bread with him in his house. They comforted him, and consoled him concerning all the evil that the LORD had brought on him. And each of them gave him a piece of money and a gold ring.

42:12 So the LORD blessed the latter end of Job more than his beginning. He had fourteen thousand sheep, six thousand camels, one thousand yoke of oxen, and a thousand female donkeys.

42:13 He had also seven sons and three daughters.

42:14 He called the name of the first, Jemimah; and the name of the second, Keziah; and the name of the third, Keren Happuch.

42:15 In all the land were no women found so beautiful as the daughters of Job. Their father gave them an inheritance among their brothers.

42:16 After this Job lived one hundred forty years, and saw his sons, and his sons' sons, to four generations.

42:17 So Job died, being old and full of days.

God leaves it up to Job as to whether his friends are to be forgiven. One can imagine that Job might be angry, but he isn't. From atop his ash heap, Job forgives his friends. Whether living in a palatial home or sitting on an ash heap, Job loves God and wants to carry out his teachings. He does not obey

God to be rewarded, he obeys God out of love. Satan has utterly failed to corrupt Job. Job is truly "a blameless and upright man."

After Job forgives his friends, God restores Job to his prominent position. Is this a reward for Job's loyalty? Maybe, but maybe it has more to do with Job's mission on earth. He still has work to do, people to help.

What does it mean that Job gave his daughters "an inheritance among their brothers"? This would have been very unusual in the ancient world. Job's suffering and grief has led him to a greater appreciation of those around him. He loves his daughters as he loves his sons and he will treat them equally, no matter what the custom of the time may be.

Job did not succumb to bitterness and hatred. Job trusts God. Job loves God. Job relies on God. Job prays to God throughout his suffering. Job realizes that he will never understand why evil things happen, but he does understand that God will never abandon him. God is always there to give him strength. The Book of Job may not fully answer the question "why bad things happen to good people?", but Job does provide an example of how good people respond to those "bad things."

FRANCIS BROWN

3. The Book of Proverbs

A proverb is a wise saying or teaching. The Book of Proverbs is a collection of 659 proverbs. The Book of Proverbs was intended to help people navigate the difficulties of this world without sacrificing the wellbeing of their souls. As we know from the Book of Job, these teachings do not guarantee that everything will work out for one's benefit. The advice given will increase one's chances for a fulfilling life.

Primary responsibility for the book is given to King Solomon who ruled in the tenth century BC.

Chapters 1-9 Prologue

The first nine chapters act as a prologue for the book. These chapters may have been added after Solomon's reign. Chapter 1 starts by giving credit for the proverbs to Solomon and stating the purpose of the book:

1:1 The proverbs of Solomon, the son of David, king of Israel:

1:2 To know wisdom and instruction, to discern the words of understanding.

1:3 To receive instruction in wise dealing, in righteousness, justice, and equity.

1:4 To give shrewdness to the inexperienced, knowledge and discretion to the young man.

1:5 A wise man will hear and increase in learning, and a man of understanding will attain to sound counsel.

1:6 To understand a proverb, and parables, the words and riddles of the wise.

1:7 The fear of the Lord is the beginning of knowledge; but the foolish despise wisdom and instruction.

1:8 My son, listen to your father's instruction, and do not forsake your mother's teaching:

1:9 for they will be a garland of grace for your head, and a necklace of honor around your neck.

Chapter 1 continues in versus 10-19 to instruct individuals not to be drawn into sin by sinners. Sinners "run to sin" and eventually are consumed by it. Chapter 1 finishes with wisdom in the form of a woman calling out, pleading for people to listen and learn for their own well-being before it is too late:

1:20 Wisdom calls aloud in the street. She utters her voice in the public squares.

1:21 She calls at the head of noisy places. At the entrance of the city gates, she utters her words:

1:22 "How long, you simple ones, will you love simplicity? How long will mockers delight themselves in mockery, and fools hate knowledge?

1:23 Turn at my reproof. Look, I will pour out my spirit on you. I will make known my words to you.

1:24 Because I have called, and you have refused; I have stretched out my hand, and no one has paid attention;

1:25 but you have ignored all my counsel, and wanted none of my reproof;

1:26 I also will laugh at your disaster. I will mock when calamity overtakes you;

1:27 when calamity overtakes you like a storm, when your disaster comes on like a whirlwind; when distress and anguish come on you.

1:28 Then will they call on me, but I will not answer. They will seek me diligently, but they will not find me;

1:29 because they hated knowledge, and did not choose the fear of the Lord.

1:30 They wanted none of my counsel. They despised all my reproof.

1:31 Therefore they will eat of the fruit of their own way, and be filled with their own schemes.

1:32 For the backsliding of the simple will kill them. The careless ease of fools will destroy them.

1:33 But whoever listens to me will dwell securely, and will be at ease, without fear of harm."

Chapter 2 teaches that God gives wisdom:

2:6 For the Lord gives wisdom. Out of his mouth comes knowledge and understanding.

2:7 He lays up sound wisdom for the upright. He is a shield to those who walk in integrity;

2:8 that he may guard the paths of justice, and preserve the way of his faithful ones.

2:9 Then you will understand righteousness and justice, equity and every good path.

2:10 For wisdom will enter into your heart. Knowledge will be pleasant to your soul.

2:11 Discretion will watch over you. Understanding will keep you.

Chapter 3 teaches that people should trust in God and not just rely on their own experiences and knowledge (as Job's friends did):

3:5 Trust in the Lord with all your heart, and do not lean on your own understanding.

3:6 In all your ways acknowledge him, and he will make your paths straight.

3:7 Do not be wise in your own eyes. Fear the Lord and depart from evil.

3:8 It will be health to your body, and nourishment to your bones.

In chapter 4, the author continues to advise the reader to seek wisdom and avoid evil:

4:1 Listen, sons, to a father's instruction. Pay attention and know understanding;

4:2 for I give you sound learning. Do not forsake my law.

4:3 For I was a son to my father, tender and an only child in the sight of my mother.

4:4 He taught me, and said to me: "Let your heart retain my words. Keep my commandments, and live.

4:5 Get wisdom. Get understanding. Do not forget, neither swerve from the words of my mouth.

4:6 Do not forsake her, and she will preserve you. Love her, and she will keep you.

4:7 Wisdom is supreme. Get wisdom. Yes, though it costs all your possessions, get understanding.

4:8 Esteem her, and she will exalt you. She will bring you to honor when you embrace her.

4:9 She will give to your head a garland of grace. She will deliver a crown of splendor to you.

4:10 Listen, my son, and receive my sayings. The years of your life will be many.

4:11 I have taught you in the way of wisdom. I have led you in straight paths.

4:12 When you go, your steps will not be hampered. When you run, you will not stumble.

4:13 Take firm hold of instruction. Do not let her go. Keep her, for she is your life.

4:14 Do not enter into the path of the wicked. Do not walk in the way of evil men.

4:15 Avoid it, and do not pass by it. Turn from it, and pass on.

4:16 For they do not sleep, unless they do evil. Their sleep is taken away, unless they make someone fall.

4:17 For they eat the bread of wickedness, and drink the wine of violence.

4:18 But the path of the righteous is like the dawning light, that shines more and more until the perfect day.

4:19 The way of the wicked is like darkness. They do not know what they stumble over.

4:20 My son, attend to my words. Turn your ear to my sayings.

4:21 Let them not depart from your eyes. Keep them in the midst of your heart.

4:22 For they are life to him who finds them, and health to all of his body.

4:23 Guard your heart with all diligence, for out of it is the wellspring of life.

4:24 Put away from yourself a perverse mouth. Put corrupt lips far from you.

4:25 Let your eyes look straight ahead. Fix your gaze directly before you.

4:26 Make the path of your feet level. Let all of your ways be established.

4:27 Do not turn to the right hand nor to the left. Remove your foot from the path of evil.

Chapter 5 teaches individuals to respect the sanctity of marriage and that nothing good comes from adultery. This teaching is reinforced in parts of chapters 6 and 7.

The first five verses in chapter 6 warn against guaranteeing the debt or obligation of a stranger or even a friend. Why? If they don't pay off the debt, you will be responsible for it and this places you at their mercy. Verses 6-11 warn against being a sluggard (sluggards are doomed to permanent poverty). Verses 12-15 warn that calamity will eventually fall on those who are wicked. Verses 16-19 list seven things the Lord hates:

6:16 There are six things which the Lord hates; yes, seven which are an abomination to him:

6:17 haughty eyes, a lying tongue, hands that shed innocent blood;

6:18 a heart that devises wicked schemes, feet that are swift in running to mischief,

6:19 a false witness who utters lies, and he who sows discord among brothers.

Chapter 6 and 7 go on to encourage the reader to keep these teachings and again warn against adultery and promiscuity because they lead to "Sheol, going down to the chambers of death."

In Chapter 8, wisdom (again in the form of a woman) pleads for people to listen. She calls out "You simple, understand prudence. You fools, be of an understanding heart." The woman goes to state that wisdom is more valuable than riches:

8:11 "For wisdom is better than rubies. All the things that may be desired can't be compared to it.

8:12 I, wisdom, have made prudence my dwelling. Find out knowledge and discretion.

8:13 The fear of the Lord is to hate evil. I hate pride, arrogance, the evil way, and the perverse mouth.

8:14 Counsel and sound knowledge are mine. I have understanding and power.

8:15 By me kings reign, and rulers decree justice."

We next learn that wisdom has been with God from the very beginning:

8:22 "The Lord created me in the beginning, before his works of old.

8:23 I was set up from everlasting, from the beginning, before the earth existed."

Wisdom is a friend, not an enemy, of mankind:

8:31 "Rejoicing in his whole world. My delight was with the sons of men.

8:32 Now therefore, son, listen to me, for blessed are those who keep my ways.

8:33 Hear instruction and be wise. Do not refuse it.

8:34 Blessed is the man who hears me, watching daily at my gates, waiting at my door posts.

8:35 For whoever finds me, finds life, and will obtain favor from the Lord.

8:36 But he who sins against me wrongs his own soul. All those who hate me love death."

Chapter 9 tells the reader that they have a chose, they can enter the house of wisdom or the house of folly. First wisdom invites people to her house for a feast:

9:1 Wisdom has built her house. She has set up her seven pillars.

9:2 She has prepared her meat. She has mixed her wine. She has also set her table.

9:3 She has sent out her maidens. She cries from the highest places of the city:

9:4 "Whoever is simple, let him turn in here." As for him who is void of understanding, she says to him,

9:5 "Come, eat some of my bread, Drink some of the wine which I have mixed.

9:6 Leave your simple ways, and live. Walk in the way of understanding.

9:7 He who corrects a mocker invites insult. He who reproves a wicked man invites abuse.

9:8 Do not reprove a scoffer, lest he hate you. Reprove a wise man, and he will love you.

9:9 Instruct a wise man, and he will be still wiser. Teach a righteous man, and he will increase in learning.

9:10 The fear of the Lord is the beginning of wisdom. The knowledge of the Holy One is understanding.

9:11 For by me your days will be multiplied. The years of your life will be increased.

9:12 If you are wise, you are wise for yourself. If you mock, you alone will bear it."

Folly, also in the form of a woman, invites people to her house:

9:13 The foolish woman is loud, undisciplined, and knows nothing.

9:14 She sits at the door of her house, on a seat in the high places of the city,

9:15 To call to those who pass by, who go straight on their ways,

9:16 "Whoever is simple, let him turn in here." As for him who is void of understanding, she says to him,

9:17 "Stolen water is sweet. Food eaten in secret is pleasant."

9:18 But he doesn't know that the dead are there, that her guests are in the depths of Sheol.

Chapters 10-24 The Proverbs of Solomon

Chapters 10-24 contain the proverbs whose inclusion in the Book of Proverbs is attributed to King Solomon. He is thought to be the primary author of some proverbs and editor of others. There are over 450 proverbs in these fifteen chapters. What follows is just a small sample of proverbs from each chapter:

Chapter10

10:3 The Lord will not allow the soul of the righteous to go hungry, but he thrusts away the desire of the wicked.

10:8 The wise in heart accept commandments, but a chattering fool will fall.

10:12 Hatred stirs up strife, but love covers all wrongs.

10:23 It is a fool's pleasure to do wickedness, but wisdom is a man of understanding's pleasure.

10:28 The prospect of the righteous is joy, but the hope of the wicked will perish.

Chapter 11

11:2 When pride comes, then comes shame, but with humility comes wisdom.

11:3 The integrity of the upright shall guide them, but the perverseness of the treacherous shall destroy them.

11:9 With his mouth the godless man destroys his neighbor, but the righteous will be delivered through knowledge.

11:12 One who despises his neighbor is void of wisdom, but a man of understanding holds his peace.

11:13 One who brings gossip betrays a confidence, but one who is of a trustworthy spirit is one who keeps a secret.

11:15 He who is collateral for a stranger will suffer for it, but he who refuses pledges of collateral is secure.

11:19 He who is truly righteous gets life. He who pursues evil gets death.

11:20 Those who are perverse in heart are an abomination to the Lord, but those whose ways are blameless are his delight.

11:27 He who diligently seeks good seeks favor, but he who searches after evil, it shall come to him.

11:28 He who trusts in his riches will fall, but the righteous shall flourish as the green leaf.

Chapter 12

12:1 Whoever loves correction loves knowledge, but he who hates reproof is stupid.

12:15 The way of a fool is right in his own eyes, but he who is wise listens to counsel.

12:16 A fool shows his annoyance the same day, but one who overlooks an insult is prudent.

12:17 He who is truthful testifies honestly, but a false witness lies.

12:21 No mischief shall happen to the righteous, but the wicked shall be filled with evil.

12:22 Lying lips are an abomination to the Lord, but those who speak the truth are his delight.

12:25 Anxiety in a man's heart weighs it down, but a kind word makes it glad.

Chapter 13

13:3 He who guards his mouth guards his soul. One who opens wide his lips comes to ruin.

13:5 A righteous man hates lies, but a wicked man brings shame and disgrace.

13:9 The light of the righteous shines brightly, but the lamp of the wicked is snuffed out.

13:20 One who walks with wise men grows wise, but a companion of fools suffers harm.

13:24 One who spares the rod hates his son, but one who loves him is careful to discipline him.

Chapter 14

14:1 Every wise woman builds her house, but the foolish one tears it down with her own hands.

14:5 A truthful witness will not lie, but a false witness pours out lies.

14:6 A scoffer seeks wisdom, and doesn't find it, but knowledge comes easily to a discerning person.

14:7 Stay away from a foolish man, for you won't find knowledge on his lips.

14:8 The wisdom of the prudent is to think about his way, but the folly of fools is deceit.

14:9 Fools mock at making atonement for sins, but among the upright there is good will.

14:10 The heart knows its own bitterness and joy; he will not share these with a stranger.

14:12 There is a way which seems right to a man, but in the end it leads to death.

14:13 Even in laughter the heart may be sorrowful, and mirth may end in heaviness.

14:14 The unfaithful will be repaid for his own ways; likewise a good man will be rewarded for his ways.

14:15 A simple man believes everything, but the prudent man carefully considers his ways.

14:16 A wise man is cautious and turns away from evil, but the fool is arrogant and reckless.

14:17 He who is quick to become angry will commit folly, and a crafty man is hated.

14:18 The simple inherit folly, but the prudent are crowned with knowledge.

14:21 He who despises his neighbor sins, but blessed is he who shows kindness to the poor.

14:22 Do they not go astray who plot evil? But love and faithfulness belong to those who plan good.

14:25 A truthful witness saves souls, but a false witness is deceitful.

14:26 In the fear of the Lord is a secure fortress, and he will be a refuge for his children.

14:29 He who is slow to anger has great understanding, but he who has a quick temper displays folly.

14:30 The life of the body is a heart at peace, but envy rots the bones.

14:31 He who oppresses the poor shows contempt for his Maker, but he who is kind to the needy honors him.

14:32 The wicked is brought down in his calamity, but the righteous has a refuge in his death.

14:33 Wisdom rests in the heart of one who has understanding, and is even made known in the inward part of fools.

Chapter 15

15:3 The eyes of the Lord are everywhere, keeping watch on the evil and the good.

15:8 The sacrifice made by the wicked is an abomination to the Lord, but the prayer of the upright is his delight.

15:9 The way of the wicked is an abomination to the Lord, but he loves him who follows after righteousness.

15:12 A scoffer doesn't love to be reproved; he will not go to the wise.

15:13 A glad heart makes a cheerful face; but an aching heart breaks the spirit.

15:16 Better is little, with the fear of the Lord, than great treasure with trouble.

15:26 The Lord detests the thoughts of the wicked, but the thoughts of the pure are pleasing.

15:27 He who is greedy for gain troubles his own house, but he who hates bribes will live.

15:30 The light of the eyes rejoices the heart. Good news gives health to the bones.

15:32 He who refuses correction despises his own soul, but he who listens to reproof gets understanding.

15:33 The fear of the Lord teaches wisdom. Before honor is humility.

Chapter 16

16:2 All the ways of a man are clean in his own eyes; but the Lord weighs the motives.

16:3 Entrust your works to the Lord, and your plans will be established.

16:4 The Lord has made everything for its own end; yes, even the wicked for the day of evil.

16:5 Everyone who is proud in heart is an abomination to the Lord: they shall certainly not be unpunished.

16:6 By mercy and truth iniquity is atoned for. By the fear of the Lord men depart from evil.

16:9 A man's heart plans his course, but the Lord directs his steps.

16:16 How much better it is to get wisdom than gold. Yes, to get understanding rather than silver.

16:17 The highway of the upright is to depart from evil. He who keeps his way preserves his soul.

16:18 Pride goes before destruction, and a haughty spirit before a fall.

16:20 He who heeds the Word finds prosperity, and blessed is he who trusts in the Lord.

16:22 Understanding is a fountain of life to one who has it, but the punishment of fools is their folly.

16:23 The heart of the wise instructs his mouth, and adds learning to his lips.

16:24 Pleasant words are a honeycomb, sweet to the soul, and health to the bones.

16:27 A worthless man devises mischief. His speech is like a scorching fire.

16:28 A perverse man stirs up strife, and a gossip separates close friends.

16:29 A man of violence entices his neighbor, and leads him in a way that is not good.

Chapter 17

17:1 Better is a dry morsel with quietness than a house full of feasting with strife.

17:3 The refining pot is for silver, and the furnace for gold, but the Lord tests the hearts.

17:5 Whoever mocks the poor reproaches his Maker. He who is glad at calamity shall not be unpunished.

17:9 He who covers an offense promotes love; but he who repeats a matter separates best friends.

17:10 A rebuke enters deeper into one who has understanding than a hundred lashes into a fool.

17:14 The beginning of strife is like breaching a dam, therefore stop contention before quarreling breaks out.

17:15 He who justifies the wicked, and he who condemns the righteous, both of them alike are an abomination to the Lord.

17:20 One who has a perverse heart doesn't find prosperity, and one who has a deceitful tongue falls into trouble.

17:22 A cheerful heart makes good medicine, but a crushed spirit dries up the bones.

17:23 A wicked man receives a bribe in secret, to pervert the ways of justice.

17:24 Wisdom is before the face of one who has understanding, but the eyes of a fool wander everywhere

17:27 He who spares his words has knowledge. He who is even tempered is a man of understanding.

17:28 Even a fool, when he keeps silent, is counted wise. When he shuts his lips, he is thought to be discerning.

Chapter 18

18:2 A fool has no delight in understanding, but only in revealing his own opinion.

18:3 When wickedness comes, contempt also comes, and with shame comes disgrace.

18:4 The words of a man's mouth are like deep waters. The fountain of wisdom is like a flowing brook.

18:5 To be partial to the faces of the wicked is not good, nor to deprive the innocent of justice.

18:6 A fool's lips come into strife, and his mouth invites beatings.

18:7 A fool's mouth is his destruction, and his lips are a snare to his soul.

18:8 The words of a gossip are like tasty morsels, and they go down into a person's innermost parts.

18:9 One who is slack in his work is brother to him who is a master of destruction.

18:10 The name of the Lord is a strong tower; the righteous run into it and are safe.

18:11 The rich man's wealth is his strong city, like an unscalable wall in his own imagination.

18:12 Before destruction the heart of man is proud, but before honor is humility.

18:13 He who gives answer before he hears, that is folly and shame to him.

18:19 A brother offended is more difficult than a fortified city; and disputes are like the bars of a fortress.

Chapter 19

19:2 It isn't good to have zeal without knowledge; nor being hasty with one's feet and missing the way.

19:3 The foolishness of man subverts his way; his heart rages against the Lord.

19:8 He who gets wisdom loves his own soul. He who keeps understanding shall find good.

19:9 A false witness shall not be unpunished. He who utters lies shall perish.

19:11 The discretion of a man makes him slow to anger. It is his glory to overlook an offense.

19:15 Slothfulness casts into a deep sleep. The idle soul shall suffer hunger.

19:16 He who keeps the commandment keeps his soul, but he who is contemptuous in his ways shall die.

19:17 He who has pity on the poor lends to the Lord; he will reward him.

19:18 Discipline your son, for there is hope; do not be a willing party to his death.

19:19 A hot-tempered man must pay the penalty, for if you rescue him, you must do it again.

19:20 Listen to counsel and receive instruction, that you may be wise in your latter end.

19:21 There are many plans in a man's heart, but the Lord's counsel will prevail.

19:22 That which makes a man to be desired is his kindness. A poor man is better than a liar.

19:23 The fear of the Lord leads to life, then contentment; he rests and will not be touched by trouble.

Chapter 20

20:1 Wine is a mocker, and beer is a brawler. Whoever is led astray by them is not wise.

20:3 It is an honor for a man to keep aloof from strife; but every fool will be quarreling.

20:9 Who can say, "I have made my heart pure. I am clean and without sin?"

20:13 Do not love sleep, lest you come to poverty. Open your eyes, and you shall be satisfied with bread.

20:15 There is gold and abundance of rubies; but the lips of knowledge are a rare jewel.

20:19 He who goes about as a tale-bearer reveals secrets; therefore do not keep company with him who opens wide his lips.

20:20 Whoever curses his father or his mother, his lamp shall be put out in blackness of darkness.

20:22 Do not say, "I will pay back evil." Wait for the Lord, and he will save you.

20:27 The spirit of man is the Lord's lamp, searching all his innermost parts.

Chapter 21

21:2 Every way of a man is right in his own eyes, but the Lord weighs the hearts.

21:3 To do righteousness and justice is more acceptable to the Lord than sacrifice.

21:4 A high look, and a proud heart, the lamp of the wicked, is sin.

21:7 The violence of the wicked will drive them away, because they refuse to do what is right.

21:8 The way of the guilty is devious, but the conduct of the innocent is upright.

21:10 The soul of the wicked desires evil; his neighbor finds no mercy in his eyes.

21:11 When the mocker is punished, the simple gains wisdom. When the wise is instructed, he receives knowledge.

21:13 Whoever stops his ears at the cry of the poor, he will also cry out, but shall not be heard.

21:15 It is joy to the righteous to do justice; but it is a destruction to evildoers.

21:16 The man who wanders out of the way of understanding shall rest in the assembly of the dead.

21:17 He who loves pleasure shall be a poor man. He who loves wine and oil shall not be rich.

21:21 He who follows after righteousness and kindness finds life, righteousness, and honor.

21:23 Whoever guards his mouth and his tongue keeps his soul from troubles.

21:24 The proud and haughty man, "scoffer" is his name; he works in the arrogance of pride.

21:25 The desire of the sluggard kills him, for his hands refuse to labor.

21:26 There are those who covet greedily all day long; but the righteous give and do not withhold.

21:27 The sacrifice of the wicked is an abomination: how much more, when he brings it with a wicked mind.

21:30 There is no wisdom nor understanding nor counsel against the Lord.

Chapter 22

22:2 The rich and the poor have this in common: The Lord is the maker of them all.

22:4 The result of humility and the fear of the Lord is wealth, honor, and life.

22:5 Thorns and snares are in the path of the wicked: whoever guards his soul stays from them.

22:6 Train up a child in the way he should go, and when he is old he will not depart from it.

22:10 Drive out the mocker, and strife will go out; yes, quarrels and insults will stop.

22:14 The mouth of an adulteress is a deep pit: he who is under the Lord's wrath will fall into it.

22:17 Turn your ear and listen to the words of the wise. Apply your heart to my teaching.

22:18 For it is a pleasant thing if you keep them within you, if all of them are ready on your lips.

22:19 That your trust may be in the Lord, I teach you today.

22:24 Do not befriend a hot-tempered man, and do not associate with one who harbors anger:

22:25 lest you learn his ways and ensnare your soul.

Chapter 23

23:4 Do not weary yourself to be rich. In your wisdom, show restraint.

23:9 Do not speak in the ears of a fool, for he will despise the wisdom of your words.

23:15 My son, if your heart is wise, then my heart will be glad, even mine:

23:16 yes, my heart will rejoice, when your lips speak what is right.

23:17 Do not let your heart envy sinners; but rather fear the Lord all the day long.

23:18 If you keep these things, there is a future and your hope will not be cut off.

23:26 My son, give me your heart; and let your eyes keep in my ways.

Chapter 24

24:1 Do not be envious of evil men; neither desire to be with them:

24:2 for their hearts plot violence, and their lips talk about mischief.

24:3 Through wisdom a house is built; by understanding it is established;

24:4 by knowledge the rooms are filled with all rare and beautiful treasure.

24:8 One who plots to do evil will be called a schemer.

24:9 The schemes of folly are sin. The mocker is detested by men.

24:13 My son, eat honey, for it is good; the droppings of the honeycomb, which are sweet to your taste.

24:14 Likewise, know that wisdom is such to your soul; if you have found it, then there will be a reward, and your hope will not be cut off.

24:15 Do not lie in wait, wicked man, against the habitation of the righteous. Do not destroy his resting place:

24:16 for a righteous man falls seven times, and rises up again; but the wicked are overthrown by calamity.

24:17 Do not rejoice when your enemy falls. Do not let your heart be glad when he is overthrown;

24:18 lest the Lord see it, and it displease him, and he turn his wrath away from him.

24:19 Do not fret yourself because of evildoers; neither be envious of the wicked:

24:20 for there will be no reward to the evil man; and the lamp of the wicked shall be snuffed out.

24:26 An honest answer is like a kiss on the lips.

24:28 Do not be a witness against your neighbor without cause. Do not deceive with your lips.

24:29 Do not say, "I will do to him as he has done to me; I will render to the man according to his work."

Chapters 25-29 More Proverbs of Solomon

Solomon came to the throne in 970 BC and reigned for 40 years. We know from 1 Kings chapter 4 that the early years of Solomon's reign were spectacular. King Solomon was famous for his wisdom and learning and is credited with writing 3000 proverbs and 1005 songs. But as time went on, Solomon lost his way and the Kingdom of Israel began to suffer.

Upon Solomon's death in 930 BC, Solomon's son Rehoboam became king and the ten northern tribes broke away and established their own kingdom in the north, keeping the name Israel. Rehaboam retained control of the two southern tribes of Judah and Benjamin. The southern kingdom took the name of Judah. Jerusalem became the capital of Judah.

In 726 BC, Hezekiah became king of Judah. He succeeded his father Ahaz who was a horrible king and a horrible individual. Hezekiah, on the other hand, would become Judah's greatest king. Throughout his life, Hezekiah would look to God and scripture as a source of wisdom and guidance. Hezekiah ordered more of Solomon's proverbs to be collected and these became chapters 25-29 of the Book of Proverbs.

Chapters 30-31 Agur and Lemuel

The author of chapter 30 is identified as Agur son of Jakeh and the author of chapter 31 is identified as King Lemuel. These are non-Israelite names that appear nowhere else in scripture and it is unknown who they were.

Proverbs attempts to help people navigate the difficulties of life. Its teachings need to be read or heard more than once. As we know from Solomon, wisdom can be lost. He seemed to have forgotten many of his own teachings. Hezekiah did not make that mistake. He made sure that he was always reminded of the wisdom contained in Scripture. The evangelist Billy Graham read one chapter of Proverbs every day for many years to help him and his ministry stay on the correct path. Wisdom must be a daily exercise. Scripture must be read repeatedly for each of us to stay on the path for a fulfilling life.

4. The Book of Ecclesiastes

Ecclesiastes is the Greco-Roman form of Qoheleth, the title of this book in Hebrew. The exact meaning of Qoheleth is unknown but is usually translated as preacher or teacher. Tradition holds that King Solomon wrote Ecclesiastes late in life but he is never mentioned by name. The style and vocabulary of the book in Hebrew point to a later date for its authorship, sometime in the fourth or third century BC. It is possible that a later author was inspired by Solomon's writings (or recorded musings) to write the book that we have now.

Chapter 1

Qoheleth is translated here as Preacher. The pessimistic tone of the book starts from the very beginning:

1:1 The words of the Preacher, the son of David, king in Jerusalem:

1:2 'Vanity of vanities," says the Preacher; "Vanity of vanities, all is vanity."

1:3 What does man gain from all his labor in which he labors under the sun?

The Preacher identifies himself again in verse 12 and goes onto lament that his search for wisdom did not alleviate his despair:

1:12 I, the Preacher, was king over Israel in Jerusalem.

1:13 I applied my heart to seek and to search out wisdom concerning all that is done under the sky. It is a heavy burden that God has given to the sons of men to be afflicted with.

1:14 I have seen all the works that are done under the sun; and look, all is vanity and a chasing after wind.

1:15 That which is crooked can't be made straight; and that which is lacking can't be counted.

1:16 I said to myself, "Look, I have obtained for myself great wisdom above all who were before me in Jerusalem. Yes, my heart has had great experience of wisdom and knowledge."

1:17 I applied my heart to know wisdom, and to know madness and folly. I perceived that this also was a chasing after wind.

1:18 For in much wisdom is much grief; and he who increases knowledge increases sorrow.

Chapter 2
Wisdom did not give the preacher the joy of fulfillment, so he seeks pleasure and great wealth.

These do not give fulfillment either. The Preacher does learn that wisdom is superior to folly:

2:13 Then I saw that wisdom excels folly, as far as light excels darkness.

2:14 The wise man's eyes are in his head, and the fool walks in darkness and yet I perceived that one event happens to them all.

The wise and the foolish both die. The Preacher goes on to lament that the labor of the wise may be undone by fools who inherit the fruits of that labor. In his despair, the Preacher realizes that the joy of fulfillment can only be had with an ongoing relationship with God:

2:24 There is nothing better for a man than that he should eat and drink, and make his soul enjoy good in his labor. This also I saw, that it is from the hand of God.

2:25 For who can eat, or who can have enjoyment, apart from him?

2:26 For to the man who pleases him, God gives wisdom, knowledge, and joy; but to the sinner he gives travail, to gather and to heap up, that he may give to him who pleases God. This also is vanity and a chasing after wind.

Chapter 3
Everything has a time and place:

3:1 For everything there is a season, and a time for every purpose under heaven:

3:2 a time to be born, and a time to die; a time to plant, and a time to pluck up that which is planted;

3:3 a time to kill, and a time to heal; a time to break down, and a time to build up;

3:4 a time to weep, and a time to laugh; a time to mourn, and a time to dance;

3:5 a time to cast away stones, and a time to gather stones together; a time to embrace, and a time to refrain from embracing;

3:6 a time to seek, and a time to lose; a time to keep, and a time to cast away;

3:7 a time to tear, and a time to sew; a time to keep silence, and a time to speak;

3:8 a time to love, and a time to hate; a time for war, and a time for peace.

The Preacher goes on to tell us other things he has learned: God has made everything beautiful in its own time; the concept of eternity is planted in people's hearts but their understanding is limited; people should respect God; events repeat themselves (there is nothing new); there will be a time when God judges the righteous and the wicked. The Preacher ends chapter 3 in another fit of pessimism by stating that animals and people have the same fate, they both die. All people can do is find happiness in their work before they die.

Chapter 4

The Preacher goes from pessimism to outright despair in chapter 4. In the first three verses, the Preacher states that people are so oppressed by their rulers that they would be better off dead. Or better yet, never been born in the first place. In verse 4, the Preacher states that most people do not work for the joy of it but work to gather wealth out of envy for their neighbor. This makes their work meaningless, like "chasing the wind." In verse 7, the Preacher states it is better for people to have companions than to work alone. Finally, chapter 4 ends with the futility of political power: "Better is a poor and wise youth than an old and foolish king who doesn't know how to receive advice anymore."(4:13). The king will eventually be replaced by someone younger, his pursuit of power was futile, like "chasing the wind."

Chapter 5

Chapter 5 begins with the Preacher telling people to approach God with care and respect:

5:1 Guard your step when you go to the house of God. To draw near to listen is better than to give the sacrifice of fools, for they do not know that they do evil.

5:2 Do not be rash with your mouth, and do not let your heart be hasty to utter anything before God; for God is in heaven, and you on earth. Therefore, let your words be few.

5:3 For as a dream comes with a multitude of cares, so a fool's speech with a multitude of words.

5:4 When you vow a vow to God, do not defer to pay it; for he has no pleasure in fools. Pay that which you vow.

5:5 It is better that you should not vow, than that you should vow and not pay.

The Preacher returns to the theme that seeking and having wealth does not bring fulfillment: "He who loves silver shall not be satisfied with silver; nor he who loves abundance, with increase: this also is vanity."(5:10)

Chapter 6

The Preacher begins by stating that God has given some people great blessings, but they do not enjoy these blessings. They cannot find fulfillment. It is better to enjoy what you have than to desire what you don't have: "Better is the sight of the eyes than the wandering of the desire. This also is vanity and a chasing after wind."(6:9)

Chapter 7

The Preacher states the importance of a good name and that sorrow brings about wisdom and understanding:

7:1 A good name is better than fine perfume; and the day of death better than the day of one's birth.

7:2 It is better to go to the house of mourning than to go to the house of feasting: for that is the end of all men, and the living should take this to heart.

7:3 Sorrow is better than laughter; for by the sadness of the face the heart is made good.

7:4 The heart of the wise is in the house of mourning; but the heart of fools is in the house of mirth.

7:5 It is better to hear the rebuke of the wise, than for a man to hear the song of fools.

7:6 For as the crackling of thorns under a pot, so is the laughter of the fool. This also is vanity.

7:7 Surely extortion makes the wise man foolish; and a bribe corrupts understanding.

7:8 Better is the end of a thing than its beginning. The patient in spirit is better than the proud in spirit.

7:9 Do not be hasty in your spirit to be angry, for anger rests in the bosom of fools.

7:10 Do not say, "Why were the former days better than these?" For you do not ask wisely about this.

7:11 Wisdom is as good as an inheritance. Yes, it is more excellent for those who see the sun.

7:12 For wisdom is a defense, even as money is a defense; but the excellency of knowledge is that wisdom preserves the life of him who has it.

In verses 15-18, the Preacher tells us to practice moderation in all things. Even an overzealous pursuit of righteousness and wisdom can become self-destructive. A person can only achieve true success by respecting God and his teachings.

The Preacher goes on to state that all men sin to some extent. His search for wisdom has taught him this and many other things but much wisdom still alludes him:

7:23 All this have I proved in wisdom. I said, "I will be wise;" but it was far from me.

7:24 That which is, is far off and exceedingly deep. Who can find it out?

7:25 I turned around, and my heart sought to know and to search out, and to seek wisdom and the scheme of things, and to know that wickedness is stupidity, and that foolishness is madness.

The Preacher continues that of all the people he has meant, only 1 in 1000 of the men and none of the women were virtuous. (Here is another clue that the Preacher is Solomon, who was often unhappy with his 700 wives.) The Preacher ends by stating that people are born virtuous, but they choose to get into trouble: "Look, this only have I found: that God made man upright; but they search for many schemes."(7:29)

Chapter 8

The Preacher turns back to wisdom and some of the things he has learned. True wisdom brightens and softens a person's face. There are limits to wisdom. Wise people cannot predict the future and many things are just beyond human comprehension. Good people sometimes suffer while wicked people prosper. When the crimes of wicked people are discovered and they are not punished, this encourages others to commit crimes. People who respect God's commands will be better off in the end. The Preacher repeats the theme of enjoying life in the moment: "Then I commended mirth, because a man has no better thing under the sun, than to eat, and to drink, and to be joyful; for that will accompany him in his labor all the days of his life which God has given him under the sun."(8:15)

Chapter 9

The Preacher repeats the theme that death comes to everyone so enjoy life while you have it. Then the Preacher states that he has learned that wisdom is better than strength:

9:13 I have also seen wisdom under the sun in this way, and it seemed great to me.

9:14 There was a little city, and few men within it; and a great king came against it, besieged it, and built great siege works against it.

9:15 Now a poor wise man was found in it, and he by his wisdom delivered the city; yet no man remembered that same poor man.

9:16 Then said I, wisdom is better than strength. Nevertheless, the poor man's wisdom is despised, and his words are not heard.

9:17 The words of the wise heard in quiet are better than the cry of him who rules among fools.

9:18 Wisdom is better than weapons of war; but one sinner destroys much good.

Even though the wise man saved the city, the foolish ruler and people of the city chose to forget him and his wisdom, undoing the good that he had done.

Chapter 10

The Preacher continues talking about folly destroying the benefits of wisdom: "Dead flies cause the oil of the perfumer to send forth an evil odor; so does a little folly outweigh wisdom and honor."(10:1)

The Preacher states that he has seen kings make the mistake of giving power to fools while ignoring the wise:

10:5 There is an evil which I have seen under the sun, the sort of error which proceeds from the ruler.

10:6 Folly is set in great dignity, and the worthy sit in a low place.

10:7 I have seen servants on horses, and princes walking like servants on the earth.

In verses 8-11, the Preacher states that there is a risk in doing a task, but wise planning and skill will help avoid mishaps and bring success.

The Preacher then returns to the danger of fools. If a kingdom is ruled by a fool, the kingdom will collapse while the king feasts and thinks money will solve all his problems. The Preacher concludes the chapter with a bit of practical advice: if you have the misfortune of having a fool for a king, don't curse him (even in private) because word of it might get back to him and that won't be good for you.

Chapter 11

11:1 Cast your bread on the waters; for you shall find it after many days.

11:2 Give a portion to seven, yes, even to eight; for you do not know what evil will be on the earth.

The meaning of these verses is often debated. One interpretation is that if you give to charity, rewards will eventually come back to you. Another interpretation is that you must take risks in life to achieve success, just don't bet everything on one venture. In other words, don't put all your eggs in one basket but instead in seven or eight baskets.

The Preacher goes on to say no matter what the weather (good or bad), a farmer must keep working. Likewise, all us must keep going. We can't predict which days will be good or bad, we can only be sure that we will have both: "Yes, if a man lives many years, let him rejoice in them all; but let him remember the days of darkness, for they shall be many. All that comes is vanity."(11:8)

The Preacher ends chapter 11 with advice for the young. Enjoy your youth but do so while respecting God and his teachings. Failure to do so will make your youth meaningless.

Chapter 12

In chapter 12, the Preacher continues to warn of a misspent youth. People should seek God's wisdom early in life in order to have a fulfilling lives. The text then goes on to describe the preacher as wise person, a person who collected proverbs, a person who taught the people, and a person who always tried to be truthful. The chapter and the book conclude with the following:

12:13 This is the end of the matter. All has been heard. Fear God and keep his commandments; for this is the whole duty of man.

12:14 For God will bring every work into judgment, with every hidden thing, whether it is good, or whether it is evil.

According to Jewish tradition, Solomon wrote the Song of Songs in his youth, Proverbs in his prime, and Ecclesiastes at the end of his life. We know from Kings chapter 11 that at some point Solomon forgot his own proverbs and repeatedly disobeyed God's commandments. Unlike Job, Solomon failed to maintain his relationship with God. This may account for the pessimism and despair that is evident in much of Ecclesiastes. Without a good relationship with God, all of life is vanity.

5. The Book of Psalms

A Psalm is a sacred poem or song. The Book of Psalms gets its name from the Greek *psalmo*s, meaning "songs sung to musical accompaniment." The Hebrew title for the book is *tehillim*, meaning "praises" or "praise-songs." The Book of Psalms contains 150 psalms divided into 5 smaller books or parts. Why they are divided into 5 parts is unknown. The dates of the individual psalms vary widely; the earliest being Psalm 90, *A prayer of Moses, the man of God*. Each psalm is an individual poem with its own subject matter and theme or themes. Some of the psalms have a clear primary theme while others do not. Scholars often group similar psalms into categories but often disagree on how some of the psalms should be classified. For instance, some sources give the number of mostly wisdom psalms in the book as 3 while other sources give a number as high as 15. The Book of Psalms that we have now was probably arranged around 400 BC. The Book of Psalms is not in chronological order.

Part 1: Psalms 1-41

The first section contains 37 psalms credited to King David and 4 psalms of anonymous authorship. The Book of Psalms opens with a psalm of wisdom by an anonymous author:

1:1 Blessed is the one who does not follow the advice of the wicked, or take the path of sinners, or join in with scoffers.

1:2 But his delight is in the law of the Lord, and on this law he meditates day and night.

1:3 He will be like a tree planted by the streams of water, that brings forth its fruit in its season, whose leaf also does not wither, and whatever he does shall prosper.

1:4 Not so with the wicked; instead, they are like the chaff which the wind drives away from the surface of the ground.

1:5 Therefore the wicked shall not stand in the judgment, nor sinners in the congregation of the righteous.

1:6 For the Lord knows the way of the righteous, but the way of the wicked shall perish.

The subject of Psalm 2, also of anonymous authorship, is the anointing and coronation of a king, in this case a messianic king. Some scholars classify the psalm as a royal psalm while others classify it as a messianic psalm. This psalm is quoted by Paul in Acts 4:25-28. There, Paul gives credit for the psalm to King David.

2:1 Why do the nations rage, and the peoples plot in vain?

2:2 The kings of the earth take a stand, and the rulers take counsel together, against the Lord, and against his Anointed:

2:3 "Let us break their shackles and throw off their ropes from us."

2:4 The one who sits in the heavens laughs. The Lord scoffs at them.

2:5 Then he will speak to them in his anger, and terrify them in his wrath:

2:6 "But I myself have installed my king on Zion, my holy hill."

2:7 I will tell of the decree. The Lord said to me, "You are my son. Today I have become your father.

2:8 Ask of me, and I will give the nations as your inheritance, and the farthest parts of the earth for your possession.

2:9 You shall rule them with an iron scepter. You shall dash them in pieces like a potter's vessel."

2:10 Now therefore, you kings, be wise; receive correction, you judges of the earth.

2:11 Serve the Lord with fear and rejoice with trembling.

2:12 Do homage in purity, lest he be angry, and you perish in the way, when his anger is suddenly kindled. Blessed are all those who take refuge in him.

Psalm 23 is probably the best known of all the psalms. It is a confidence or trust psalm in which King David places his trust in God:

A Psalm by David

23:1 The Lord is my shepherd; I lack nothing.

23:2 He makes me lie down in green pastures. He leads me beside still waters.

23:3 He restores my soul. He guides me in the paths of righteousness for his name's sake.

23:4 Even though I walk through the valley of the shadow of death, I will fear no evil, for you are with me. Your rod and your staff, they comfort me.

23:5 You prepare a table before me in the presence of my enemies. You anoint my head with oil. My cup runs over.

23:6 Surely goodness and loving kindness shall follow me all the days of my life, and I will dwell in the Lord's house forever.

Part 2: Psalms 42-72

The second section contains 19 psalms credited to King David, 7 credited to the sons of Korah, 1 credited to Solomon, 1 to Asaph, and 3 are anonymous. The sons of Korah were musicians and singers in the royal court. Asaph was the chief leader of the Temple choir and served both King David and King Solomon.

Psalm 47 is an example of an enthronement psalm proclaiming God's rule over the earth. The term Selah in verse 4 is a direction for the choir and is thought to mean pause or interlude.

For the Chief Musician. A Psalm by the sons of Korah.

47:1 Oh clap your hands, all you nations. Shout to God with the voice of triumph.

47:2 For the Lord Most High is awesome. He is a great King over all the earth.

47:3 He subdues nations under us, and peoples under our feet.

47:4 He chooses our inheritance for us, the glory of Jacob whom he loved. Selah.

47:5 God has gone up with a shout, the Lord with the sound of a trumpet.

47:6 Sing praise to God, sing praises. Sing praises to our King, sing praises.

47:7 For God is the King of all the earth. Sing praises with understanding.

47:8 God reigns over the nations. God sits on his holy throne.

47:9 The princes of the peoples are gathered together, the people of the God of Abraham. For the shields of the earth belong to God. He is greatly exalted.

Psalm 54 is an example of a lament psalm. There are more psalms of lament in the Book of Psalms than any other type.

For the Chief Musician. On stringed instruments. A contemplation by David, when the Ziphites came and said to Saul, "Isn't David hiding himself among us?"

54:1 Save me, God, by your name. Vindicate me in your might.

54:2 Hear my prayer, God. Listen to the words of my mouth.

54:3 For strangers have risen up against me. Violent men have sought after my soul. They haven't set God before them. Selah.

54:4 Look, God is my helper. The Lord is the one who sustains my soul.

54:5 He will repay the evil to my enemies. Destroy them in your truth.

54:6 With a free will offering, I will sacrifice to you. I will give thanks to your name, Lord, for it is good.

54:7 For he has delivered me out of all trouble. My eye has seen triumph over my enemies.

Psalm 67 is usually considered a blessing or thanksgiving psalm since it expresses the gratefulness of Israel to God for his guidance and blessings:

For the Chief Musician. With stringed instruments. A Psalm. A song.

67:1 May God be merciful to us, bless us, and cause his face to shine on us. Selah (interlude)

67:2 That your way may be known on earth, and your salvation among all nations,

67:3 let the peoples praise you, God. Let all the peoples praise you.

67:4 Let the nations be glad and sing for joy, for you will judge the world in righteousness. You will judge the peoples with equity and guide the nations on earth.

67:5 Let the peoples praise you, God. Let all the peoples praise you.

67:6 The earth has yielded its increase. God, even our own God, will bless us.

67:7 God will bless us. Every part of the earth shall fear him.

Part 3: Psalms 73-89

The third section contains 11 psalms credited to Asaph, 4 to the sons of Korah, 1 to King David, and 1 to Ethan the Ezrahite. Ethan the Ezrahite is mentioned in 1 Kings 4:31 as being famous for his wisdom; that is the only fact that we know about him.

Psalm 73 is a wisdom psalm by Asaph. In this psalm, we learn that Asaph has become embittered at seeing wicked people become successful. He has always tried to do what is right and has suffered for it. In verse 15, he states that he could have gone along with the wicked but in doing so, he would have betrayed God and his people. He tries to understand this injustice but fails. Then Asaph reconnects with God, perhaps by actually visiting the Temple or just opening his heart to God. Asaph realizes that God's justice will in the end prevail. In verses 21 and 22, Asaph states he has allowed his ignorance to "embitter his heart and grieve his soul." He has been envious of the success of the wicked. He now realizes that his relationship with God is far more important. God has been with him all the time, guiding him, supporting him. It is better to be close to God than to imitate the wicked.

A Psalm by Asaph.
73:1 Surely God is good to Israel, to those who are pure in heart.

73:2 But as for me, my feet were almost gone. My steps had nearly slipped.

73:3 For I was envious of the arrogant, when I saw the prosperity of the wicked.

73:4 For there are no struggles in their death, and their strength is firm.

73:5 They are free from burdens of men, neither are they plagued like other men.

73:6 Therefore pride is like a chain around their neck. Violence covers them like a garment.

73:7 Their sin proceeds forth from fatness. Their hearts overflow with imaginations.

73:8 They scoff and speak with malice. In arrogance, they threaten oppression.

73:9 They have set their mouth against the heavens. Their tongue walks through the earth.

73:10 Therefore my people turn to them, and they drink up waters of abundance.

73:11 They say, "How does God know? Is there knowledge in the Most High?"

73:12 Look, these are the wicked. Being always at ease, they increase in riches.

73:13 Surely in vain I have cleansed my heart, and washed my hands in innocence,

73:14 For all day long have I been plagued, and punished every morning.

73:15 If I had said, "I will speak thus," look, I would have betrayed the generation of your children.

73:16 When I tried to understand this, it was too painful for me;

73:17 Until I entered God's sanctuary and considered their latter end.

73:18 Surely you set them in slippery places. You throw them down to destruction.

73:19 How they are suddenly destroyed. They are completely swept away with terrors.

73:20 As a dream when one wakes up, so, Lord, when you awake, you will despise their fantasies.

73:21 For my soul was grieved. I was embittered in my heart.

73:22 I was so senseless and ignorant. I was a brute beast before you.

73:23 Nevertheless, I am continually with you. You have held my right hand.

73:24 You will guide me with your counsel, and afterward receive me to glory.

73:25 Who do I have in heaven? There is no one on earth who I desire besides you.

73:26 My flesh and my heart fails, but God is the strength of my heart and my portion forever.

73:27 For, look, those who are far from you shall perish. You have destroyed all those who are unfaithful to you.

73:28 But it is good for me to come close to God. I have made the Lord my refuge, that I may tell of all your works in the gates of the daughter of Zion.

Psalm 87 is an example of a psalm of Zion or Jerusalem. This type of psalm proclaims the glory of Jerusalem:

A Psalm by the sons of Korah; a Song.
87:1 His foundation is in the holy mountains.
87:2 The Lord loves the gates of Zion more than all the dwellings of Jacob.
87:3 Glorious things are spoken about you, city of God. Selah.
87:4 I will record Rahab and Babylon among those who acknowledge me. Look, Philistia, Tyre, and also Ethiopia: "This one was born there."
87:5 Yes, of Zion it will be said, "This one and that one was born in her;" the Most High himself will establish her.
87:6 The Lord will count, when he writes up the peoples, "This one was born there." Selah.
87:7 Those who sing as well as those who dance say, "All my springs are in you."

Part 4: Psalms 90-106

The fourth section contains 2 psalms credited to King David, 1 to Moses, and 14 are anonymous.
The title of Psalm 100 is translated here as a Psalm of Thanksgiving, but the title is given as A Psalm of Praise in many translations.

A Psalm of Thanksgiving.
100.2 Shout for joy to the Lord, all you lands.
100:2 Serve the Lord with gladness. Come before his presence with singing.

100:3 Know that the Lord, he is God. It is he who has made us, and not we ourselves. We are his people, and the sheep of his pasture.

100:4 Enter into his gates with thanksgiving, and into his courts with praise. Give thanks to him and bless his name.

100:5 For the Lord is good. His loving kindness endures forever, and his faithfulness to all generations.

Part 5: Psalms 107-150

The final section contains 15 psalms credited to King David, 1 to Solomon, and 38 are anonymous.

Psalm 123 is an example of psalm of pilgrimage sung by pilgrims as they traveled (or ascended) to Jerusalem:

A Song of Ascents.

123.1 To you I do lift up my eyes, you who sit in the heavens.

123:2 Look, as the eyes of servants look to the hand of their master, as the eyes of a maid to the hand of her mistress; so our eyes look to the Lord, our God, until he has mercy on us.

123:3 Have mercy on us, Lord, have mercy on us, for we have endured much contempt.

123:4 Our soul is exceedingly filled with the scoffing of those who are at ease, with the contempt of the proud.

The Book of Psalms closes with Psalm 150, a psalm of praise:

150:1 Praise the Lord. Praise God in his sanctuary. Praise him in his heavens for his acts of power.

150:2 Praise him for his mighty acts. Praise him according to his excellent greatness.

150:3 Praise him with the sounding of the trumpet. Praise him with harp and lyre.

150:4 Praise him with tambourine and dancing. Praise him with stringed instruments and flute.

150:5 Praise him with loud cymbals. Praise him with resounding cymbals.

150:6 Let everything that has breath praise the Lord. Praise the Lord.

We know that fools are often destroyed by their emotions. The wise can also be brought down by their emotions. The Preacher in Ecclesiastes is overwhelmed by the injustices and pain in his world. Likewise, we see in Psalm 73 that Asaph is overwhelmed by the ongoing success of the wicked. Asaph, however, is brought out of his despair by reconnecting with God. Asaph realized that true wisdom is not just an intellectual pursuit but an emotional one as well. He realized it is important to have what we would call "emotional intelligence." The Book of Psalms shows us that to manage our emotions, we must share our emotions with God through song and prayer. There are times when we need to talk to God for emotional peace and strength.

6. The Song of Solomon

The Song of Solomon (or the Song of Songs) is a collection of ancient Hebrew love poems. The first verse of the book gives credit to Solomon who may have written the poems or more likely adapted and arranged them into this work. Further changes were probably made in the centuries following Solomon. The Song of Solomon is basically a love song (or a series of love songs) sung by a young man, a young woman, and the companions of the woman. This work was extremely popular in ancient Israel. Like today's love songs, the words were probably chosen more for their emotional impact and rhyming ability than for their literal meaning, making this work very difficult to translate and interpret. Because of this, translations of this work differ.

The book opens with a young woman or maiden longing for the embrace of her love:

1:1 The Song of songs, which is Solomon's.

Young woman:

1:2 Let him kiss me with the kisses of his mouth; for your love is better than wine.

1:3 Your oils have a pleasing fragrance. Your name is oil poured forth, therefore the virgins love you.

1:4 Take me away with you. Let us hurry. The king has brought me into his chambers.

The companions, the daughters of Jerusalem:

We will be glad and rejoice in you. We will praise your love more than wine.

Young woman:

1:5 I am dark, but lovely, you daughters of Jerusalem, like Kedar's tents, like Solomon's curtains.

1:6 Do not stare at me because I am dark, because the sun has scorched me. My mother's sons were angry with me. They made me keeper of the vineyards. I haven't kept my own vineyard.

1:7 Tell me, you whom my soul loves, where you graze your flock, where you rest them at noon; For why should I be as one who is veiled beside the flocks of your companions?

The young woman's love, a young man identified here as shepherd, responds:

Young man:

1:8 If you do not know, most beautiful among women, follow the tracks of the sheep. Graze your young goats beside the shepherds' tents.

1:9 I have compared you, my love, to a steed in Pharaoh's chariots.

1:10 Your cheeks are beautiful with earrings, your neck with strings of jewels.

1:11 We will make you earrings of gold, with studs of silver.

Young woman:

1:12 While the king sat at his table, my perfume spread its fragrance.

1:13 My beloved is to me a sachet of myrrh, that lies between my breasts.

1:14 My beloved is to me a cluster of henna blossoms from the vineyards of En-Gedi.

Young man:

1:15 Look, you are beautiful, my love. Look, you are beautiful. Your eyes are doves.

Young woman:

1:16 Look, you are beautiful, my beloved, yes, pleasant; and our couch is verdant.

Young man:

1:17 The beams of our house are cedars. Our rafters are firs.

The young man is Solomon. At one time, Solomon was just one of the many sons of King David and not particularly important. Perhaps the maiden knew Solomon before he became King or is just making the point that she loves him not as a king but for the man he is. For his part, the young man (Solomon) loves the maiden even though she has neglected her beauty, having a rather hard life with her family.

The young man and woman long to be with each other. But the young woman knows they are not ready to be together. She asks her friends in 2:7 and

3:5 not to encourage the relationship until it is time to "awaken love."

Chapter 3 ends with the young woman's companions seeing the wedding procession of Solomon as he comes to marry his love:

The daughters of Jerusalem:
3:6 Who is this who comes up from the wilderness like pillars of smoke, perfumed with myrrh and frankincense, with all spices of the merchant?

3:7 Look, it is Solomon's carriage. Sixty mighty men are around it, of the mighty men of Israel.

3:8 They all handle the sword and are expert in war. Every man has his sword on his thigh, because of fear in the night.

3:9 King Solomon made himself a carriage of the wood of Lebanon.

3:10 He made its pillars of silver, its bottom of gold, its seat of purple, its midst being paved with love, from the daughters of Jerusalem.

3:11 Go forth, you daughters of Zion, and see King Solomon, with the crown with which his mother has crowned him, on the day of his wedding, on the day of the gladness of his heart.

In chapter 4, the marriage is consummated. The marriage is a strong union. But in chapters 6, there is a separation of some sort. Solomon may have been busy with his duties or the young woman may have been called away by her family. Perhaps the separation is not a physical one but a spiritual one. Either way, the companions call for the young woman's return in 6:13. It is in this verse that the young woman is identified as the maid of Shulam or as a Shulamite.

The separation ends in chapter 7 and the couple once again speak of their love and desire for one another. The power of the couple's love, and love in general, is spoken of in chapter 8:

8:6 Set me as a seal on your heart, as a seal on your arm; for love is strong as death. Jealousy is as cruel as Sheol. Its flashes are flashes of fire, a very flame of the Lord.

8:7 Many waters can't quench love, nor can floods drown it. If a man would give all his wealth for love, he would be utterly scorned.

True love can't be bought. The Song of Solomon ends with a simple but loving exchange:

Young man:
8:13 You who dwell in the gardens, with friends in attendance, let me hear your voice.
Young Woman:
8:14 Come away, my beloved. Be like a gazelle or a young stag on the mountains of spices.

King Solomon struggled his entire adult life to keep the Kingdom of Israel unified and at peace with its neighbors. To this end, Solomon had 700 hundred wives as marriage was a way to form political alliances. There may have been one marriage out of the 700 that was not done for political reasons.

The marriage described in the Song of Solomon is not a marriage of convenience. This is a marriage of a man and a woman who want to be together. They love each other. They respect each other. They care deeply for one another. It is a spiritual union as well as a physical one. It is no wonder that people throughout the centuries have been moved by such a powerful statement on the bond between a man and a woman united in marriage.

7. The Wisdom of Solomon

The Wisdom of Solomon (also known as the Book of Solomon or Book of Wisdom) is one of two wisdom books in the Apocrypha or Deuterocanonical books. It was written by an unknown Jewish author in Alexandria Egypt, probably in the latter part of the 1st century BC. The author wrote the book in the name of King Solomon, writing in the persona of Solomon himself. The Wisdom of Solomon is the only wisdom book originally written in Greek. The book was written at a time when the large Jewish community in Alexandria was being oppressed and Hellenistic culture was dominate. New ideas and religions were competing for followers and many left the Jewish faith. The author wrote the Wisdom of Solomon to reaffirm the Hebrew faith, to both keep and attract new adherents. He incorporated new ideas of the time (such as a clear distinction between the body and the soul) without compromising the core tenants of his faith. Scholars generally divide the book into 3 parts according to subject matter.

Part 1: Chapters 1-6:21

The first part of the book links wisdom with people's destinies. The major recurrent theme of the book is true wisdom is associated with God. Wisdom is the only source of good. To know wisdom is to gain eternal life.

Chapter 1

In the ancient world, it was necessary for a king to possess wisdom to be successful. To this end, the book opens by telling kings (judges of the earth) to love righteousness, to "think of the Lord with a good mind, seek him in singleness of heart." Why? The wicked are separated from God because wisdom will have nothing to do with them: "Because wisdom will not enter into a soul that devises evil, nor dwell in a body that is enslaved by sin."(1:4)

Because of this separation, the wicked will know death:

1:12 Don't court death in the error of your life; and don't draw destruction upon yourselves by the works of your hands,

1:13 because God didn't make death, neither does he delight when the living perish.

1:14 For he created all things that they might have being. The generative powers of the world are wholesome, and there is no poison of destruction in them, nor has death have royal dominion upon earth;

1:15 For righteousness is immortal,

1:16 but ungodly men by their hands and their words summon death; deeming him a friend, they pined for him. They made a covenant with him, because they are worthy to belong with him.

Chapter 2

Because the wicked lack wisdom, they seek pleasure and take joy in oppressing the innocent, the defenseless. The wicked hate the righteous and wish to destroy them. The wicked belong to the devil, not to God:

2:21 Thus they reasoned, and they were led astray; for their wickedness blinded them,

2:22 and they didn't know the mysteries of God, neither did they hope for wages of holiness, nor did they discern that there is a prize for blameless souls.

2:23 Because God created man for incorruption, and made him an image of his own everlastingness;

2:24 but death entered into the world by the envy of the devil, and those who belong to him experience it.

Chapter 3

The wicked may do harm on earth but they will perish. A different fate awaits the righteous: "the souls of the righteous are in the hand of God, and no torment will touch them."(3:1)

Chapter 4

Here the author stresses the importance of people protecting their virtue. Virtuous people help others escape evil by setting an example as to how to live. Virtue helps people avoid being entrapped by evil: "For the witchcraft of evil obscures the things which are good, and the whirl of desire perverts an innocent mind."(4:12)

Chapter 5

In chapter 2 the wicked persecute the righteous, but here the righteous stand in "great boldness" and face the wicked. When the wicked see the strength of the righteous, they become afraid. They begin to realize that their lack of virtue has left them without hope, without God:

5:14 Because the hope of the ungodly man is like chaff carried by the wind, as foam vanishing before a tempest; and is scattered like smoke by the wind, and passes by as the remembrance of a guest that waits but a day.

5:15 But the righteous live forever. Their reward is in the Lord, their care with the Most High.

Chapter 6

This chapter opens by once again reminding kings to seek the Lord and gain wisdom. If they don't, they will be punished. God does not treat kings differently from other people: "For the Sovereign Lord of all will not be impressed with anyone, neither will he show deference to greatness; because it is he who made both small and great, and cares about them all."(6:7)

Part 2: 6:22-11:1

The second part of the book deals with the nature of wisdom and King Solomon's pursuit of wisdom.

The author (writing as King Solomon) states: "But what wisdom is, and how she came into being, I will declare. I won't hide mysteries from you; but I will explore from her first beginning, bring the knowledge of her into clear light, and I will not pass by the truth."(6:22)

Chapter 7

Solomon is mortal, born the same way as all people. Though he is of noble birth, Solomon (like everyone else) is not born wise. He prays and understanding is given to him, the spirit of wisdom comes to him. Wisdom (depicted as a woman) is powerful because "she is a breath of the power of God, and a clear effluence of the glory of the Almighty."(7:25)

Chapters 8 and 9

The author talks about the power and beauty of wisdom. The teachings of wisdom are essential for "if a man loves righteousness, the fruits of wisdom's labor are virtues, for she teaches self-control, understanding, justice, and courage. There is nothing in life more profitable for people than these."(8:7)

Chapter 8 ends with the author introducing what is known as Solomon's Prayer for Wisdom:

8:21 But perceiving that I could not otherwise possess wisdom unless God gave her to me—yes, and to know and understand by whom the grace is given—I pleaded with the Lord and implored him, and with my whole heart I said:

Solomon's Prayer for Wisdom

9:1 "O God of the fathers, and Lord of mercy, who made all things by your word;

9:2 and by your wisdom you formed man, that he should have dominion over the creatures that were made by you,

9:3 and rule the world in holiness and righteousness, and execute judgement in uprightness of soul;

9:4 give me wisdom, her who sits by you on your thrones. Don't reject me from among your servants,

9:5 because I am your servant and the son of your handmaid, a weak and short-lived man, with little power to understand judgement and laws.

9:6 For even if a man is perfect among the sons of men, if the wisdom that comes from you is not with him, he will count for nothing.

9:7 You chose me to be king of your people, and a judge for your sons and daughters.

9:8 You gave a command to build a sanctuary on your holy mountain, and an altar in the city where you pitch your tent, a copy of the holy tent which you prepared from the beginning.

9:9 Wisdom is with you and knows your works, and was present when you were making the world, and understands what is pleasing in your eyes, and what is right according to your commandments.

9:10 Send her from the holy heavens and ask her to come from the throne of your glory; that being present with me she may work, and I may learn what pleases you well.

9:11 For she knows all things and understands, and she will guide me soberly in my actions. She will guard me in her glory.

9:12 Then my works will be acceptable. I will judge your people righteously, and I will be worthy of my father's throne.

9:13 For what man will know the counsel of God? Or who will conceive what the Lord wills?

9:14 For the thoughts of mortals are unstable, and our plans are prone to fail.

9:15 For a corruptible body weighs down the soul. The earthy frame lies heavy on a mind that is full of cares.

9:16 We can hardly guess the things that are on earth, and we find the things that are close at hand with labor; but who has traced out the things that are in the heavens?

9:17 Who gained knowledge of your counsel, unless you gave wisdom, and sent your holy spirit from on high?

9:18 It was thus that the ways of those who are on earth were corrected, and men were taught the things that are pleasing to you. They were saved through wisdom."

Chapter 10

This chapter gives examples from Israel's history when wisdom provided salvation: wisdom came to the aid of Adam and Eve after their transgression; wisdom saved Noah from the flood; wisdom recognized Abraham as a righteous man and kept him strong; wisdom rescued Lot; wisdom guided Jacob and gave him knowledge of "holy things";

wisdom entered into the soul of Moses and delivered a "holy people" from a nation of oppressors.

Part 3: 11:1-19:22

The last part deals primarily with the Exodus. The Wisdom of Solomon was written at a time when the Jewish population in Alexandria was being oppressed and many Jews were abandoning their faith for pagan gods. The author looks back to another time when Jews were being oppressed in Egypt and the Egyptian gods of that time seemed powerful.

Chapter 11

Wisdom, working through Moses, leads the Jews out of Egypt into the wilderness. There, God provides water out of a rock. This is in contrast to when God punished the Egyptians by making the Nile flow with blood. This, the first plague in Exodus, showed the powerlessness of Apis, the Egyptian god of the Nile. In 11:7, the author reminds the reader that it was in the Nile that Pharaoh ordered all the newborn Hebrew male infants to be drowned (Exodus 1:22).

In 11:15, God is repulsed by the Egyptian practice of worshiping animal like gods such as the god Heqet, the frog-headed goddess of birth. Frogs were considered sacred by Egyptians and were not to be killed. The second plague in exodus is the plague of frogs. Though this plague was horrible, the author points out in the succeeding verses that it could have been much worse. God loves all living things. The Egyptians had bought these plagues on themselves by not freeing the Hebrews.

Chapter 12
The author turns his attention to the Canaanites. The Canaanites practiced killing children as sacrifices to their gods. God found this and other aspects of their society to be an abomination, but he still showed them mercy by giving them many chances to repent.

Chapters 13-15
These chapters make the case against idolatry. Ignorant fools worship idols. Only God is worthy of worship:

15:1 But you, our God, are gracious and true, patient, and in mercy ordering all things.

15:2 For even if we sin, we are yours, knowing your dominion; but we will not sin, knowing that we have been accounted yours.

15:3 For to be acquainted with you is perfect righteousness, and to know your dominion is the root of immortality.

Chapter 15 ends with describing the Egyptians (the oppressors of the Hebrews) as fools for thinking their idols were gods.

Chapters 16-19
The author returns to the Exodus, Gods punishment of the Egyptians, and God's protection of the Hebrews. He refers again to the plague of frogs and

contrasts this to how God sent quail to feed the Israelites in the wilderness. The author then continues to describe the other plagues and contrast these to occasions when God helped his followers.

In 16:5-14, the author talks about punishing the Israelites in the wilderness with poisonous snakes (Numbers 21:4-9) for their rebellion. When the Israelites went to Moses and asked him to pray to God on their behalf for forgiveness, God forgave them. When the plagues of gnats and flies struck the Egyptians, the Egyptian gods were again powerless. If the Egyptians had just repented and obeyed God's command to free the Hebrews, they too would have been spared.

In 16:15-29, the author contrasts the plague of hail destroying the Egyptian's crops with God giving manna to the Israelites in the wilderness.

In 17:1-18:4, the author compares the plague of darkness with the pillar of fire used to lead the Israelites out of Egypt.

In 18:5-18:29, the author compares the death of the Egyptian firstborn with the aforementioned killing of the Hebrew male infants.

In 19:1-19:21, the author compares the parting of the Red Sea to save the Israelites and the destruction of the Egyptian army in the same sea.

Chapter 19 and the book ends with the following:

19:22 For in all things, O Lord, you magnified your people, and you glorified them and didn't lightly regard them, standing by their side in every time and place.

8. Ecclesiasticus or
The Wisdom of Sirach

Ecclesiasticus is the second wisdom book of the Apocrypha or Deuterocanonical books. It was written by Jesus Ben Sira (Sirach in Greek) around 180 B.C. Ben Sira wrote the book in Hebrew and his grandson translated it into Greek around 132 B.C. The translation was done in Alexandria, Egypt. This translation was included in the Septuagint and it is the grandson's translation that has been studied throughout the centuries. The original Hebrew version fell into disuse. Nothing is known about Sirach beyond what his grandson tells us in the prologue to the translation, but he was probably a wisdom teacher at one of the Jewish academies in Jerusalem.

Ecclesiasticus is more of a collection of essays or treatises than a book with a structured content. It most resembles the Book of Proverbs but is much longer, in fact it is the longest of the wisdom books.

Translations of this work vary because of additions made in the centuries after the grandson's original translation.

The prologue by Sirach's grandson to the Greek translation:

WHEREAS many and great things have been delivered to us by the law and the prophets, and by the others that have followed in their steps, for which we must give Israel the praise for instruction and wisdom; and since not only the readers need to become skillful themselves, but also those who love learning must be able to profit those who are outside, both by speaking and writing; my grandfather Jesus, having much given himself to the reading of the law, and the prophets, and the other books of our fathers, and having gained great familiarity with them, was also drawn on himself to write somewhat pertaining to instruction and wisdom, in order that those who love learning, and are devoted to these things, might make progress much more by living according to the law. You are entreated therefore to read with favor and attention, and to pardon us, if in any parts of what we have labored to interpret, we may seem to fail in some of the phrases. For things originally spoken in Hebrew don't have the same force in them when they are translated into another language. Not only these, but the law itself, and the prophecies, and the rest of the books, have no small difference, when they are spoken in their original language. For having come into Egypt in the thirty-eighth year of Energetes the king, and having continued there some time, I found a copy giving no small instruction. I thought it therefore most necessary for me to apply some diligence and travail to translate this book, applying indeed much watchfulness and skill in that space of time to bring the book to an end and publish for them also, who in the land of their travels are desiring to learn, preparing their character in advance, so as to live according to the law.

The book opens with a wisdom poem and the statement that God is the source of wisdom: "All wisdom comes from the Lord, and is with him forever." People gain wisdom by respecting God and his teachings.

Chapter 2 tells us that if we choose to serve God (and thus gain wisdom), we must prepare our souls and trust in God for it will not be easy:

2:1 My son, if you come to serve the Lord, prepare your soul for temptation.

2:2 Set your heart aright, constantly endure, and don't make haste in time of calamity.

2:3 Cling to him, and don't depart, that you may be increased at your latter end.

Chapter 3 tells us to honor our father and mother and the importance of humility:

3:3 He who honors his father will make atonement for sins.

3:4 He that gives glory to his mother is as one who lays up treasure.

Importance of humility:

3:17 My son, go on with your business in humility; so you will be loved by those acceptable to God.

3:18 The greater you are, humble yourself the more, and you will find favor before the Lord.

3:20 For the power of the Lord is great, and he is glorified by those who are lowly.

3:21 Don't seek things that are too hard for you, and don't search out things that are above your strength.

3:22 Think about the things that have been commanded of you, for you have no need of the things that are kept secret.

3:23 Don't be overly busy in your superfluous works, for more things are showed to you than men can understand.

3:24 For the conceit of many has led them astray. Evil opinion has caused their judgement to slip.

3:25 There is no light without eyes. There is no wisdom without knowledge.

3:26 A stubborn heart will do badly at the end. He who loves danger will perish in it.

3:27 A stubborn heart will be burdened with troubles. The sinner will heap sin upon sins.

3:28 The calamity of the proud is no healing, for a weed of wickedness has taken root in them.

The first verses of chapter 4 tell us not to ignore the plight of those who are in need; respect those who are wise (those who are "great"); listen to the poor and always answer them with humility and respect; seek justice for the innocent and the guilty: "Deliver him who is wronged from the hand of him that wrongs him; Don't be faint-hearted in giving judgement."(4:9)

Chapter 4 goes on to tells us the great reward and opportunity that wisdom offers us:

4:11 Wisdom exalts her sons, and takes hold of those who seek her.

4:12 He who loves her loves life. Those who seek her early will be filled with gladness.

4:13 He who holds her fast will inherit glory

Chapter 4 concludes by warning against cowardice in following wisdom's teachings. Society will try to shame you into conforming and abandoning what you know to be correct. Don't give in to evil. God will help you: "Strive for the truth to death, and the Lord God will fight for you." (4:28)

Chapter 5 warns against trying to rely on yourself (your wealth, intelligence, etc.) to make it through life. Instead, you must rely on the Lord and his teachings. Everyone makes mistakes, but God is merciful to those who seek him. However, don't keep sinning thinking you can ask for his mercy later and escape punishment. God cannot be fooled, he knows your heart.

In Chapter 6, Sirach warns against letting passion destroy your soul:

6:2 Don't exalt yourself in the counsel of your soul, that your soul be not torn in pieces as by a bull.

6:3 You will eat up your leaves, destroy your fruit, and leave yourself as a dry tree.

6:4 A wicked soul will destroy him who has it and will make him a laughing stock to his enemies.

Chapter 7 gives advice as what to do and not do. Do not commit evil acts as evil will overtake and destroy you. Do not seek power and fame as arrogance will destroy one's integrity. Do not keep repeating a sin. Pray with all of your heart but do not keep repeating yourself in prayer. Do not neglect charity. Do not laugh at another person's troubles. Do not desire to lie. Do not hate hard work. Always be humble. Do not betray a friendship for money. Do not marry a person you do not respect and always listen to and cherish a wise spouse. Treat honest and faithful servants and workers with respect. Raise your children with discipline and wisdom. Only give your daughter's hand in marriage to a man of understanding. Help the poor and sick. Support those who mourn by mourning with them. Above all else, respect God.

Chapter 8 gives advice on how to deal with people. Do not to enter into quarrels you cannot win. Do not be belligerent nor engage with a belligerent man. Do not make fun of someone for their lack of education or sophistication. Do not condemn a repentant man for a past sin for we all have sinned. Honor the elderly. Never rejoice in someone's death. Listen to the wise. Listen to the elderly. Don't encourage a sinner in his sin, his sin may destroy you as well as him. Don't let rude or obnoxious people upset you, engaging them will only harm you. Don't lend money to people more powerful than you, they won't pay you back. Don't guarantee a loan that you cannot pay yourself. Avoid reckless people. Avoid angry people. Do not confide in a fool for he will not keep your secret. Do or say nothing in the presence of a stranger that you want kept secret. Don't open your heart or speak your mind to everybody, it is often best to keep your thoughts to yourself.

Chapter 9 begins by giving advice about a man's relationship with women. Do not be jealous of the wife of your heart, jealously only brings evil. Never give your soul to a woman. Do not associate with prostitutes or other women who make their living by tempting men. Do not lust after virgins (or girls). Do not spend your time lusting after beautiful women. Never dine or drink with another's man wife, never put yourself in a situation that could lead to adultery.

Chapter 9 continues with advice on friends and neighbors. Never forsake an old friend for a new friend. Never envy the honor given a sinner for you do not know what their ultimate end will be. Never delight in the pleasures of the ungodly, they will be punished. Keep far away from a violent man but if you have to come near him, be careful and do not offend him. Let your companions be only those who respect God.

Chapter 10 (and the very end of chapter 9) gives the attributes of wise leaders. A wise leader is not reckless in their speech, they choose their words carefully. A wise leader is not talkative. A wise leader educates his people. A wise leader is not arrogant, for arrogance brings sin:

10:12 It is the beginning of pride when a man departs from the Lord. His heart has departed from him who made him.

10:13 For the beginning of pride is sin. He who keeps it will pour out abomination. For this cause the Lord brought upon them strange calamities and utterly overthrew them.

10:14 The Lord cast down the thrones of rulers and set the meek in their place.

10:15 The Lord plucked up the roots of nations and planted the lowly in their place.

Chapter 10 concludes with a discussion of honor. Honor is not given to an individual because of their social status, education, or accomplishments. Honor is given to those who respect God.

Chapter 11 begins by telling us not to judge people by their outward appearance:

11:1 The wisdom of a lowly man will lift up his head, and make him sit in the midst of great men.

11:2 Don't commend a man for his beauty. Don't abhor a man for his outward appearance.

11:3 The bee is little among flying creatures, but what it produces is the best of confections.

11:4 Don't boast about the clothes you wear, and don't exalt yourself when given honors; for the

Lord's works are wonderful, and his works are hidden among men.

Chapter 11 then continues with a warning about putting too much trust in wealth. Wealth can disappear in an instance. The chapter ends with a warning about inviting evildoers into your home:

11:33 Beware of an evildoer, for he plans wicked things, he desires to ruin your reputation.

11:34 Receive a stranger into your house, and he will cause trouble for you and estrange you from your family.

Chapter 12 tells us to help people but know who you are helping:

12:1 If you do good, know to whom you do it, and your good deeds will have thanks.

12:2 Do good to a godly man, and you will find a reward— if not from him, then from the Most High.

12:3 No good will come to him who continues to do evil, nor to him who gives no alms.

12:4 Give to the godly man, and don't help the sinner.

12:5 Do good to one who is lowly. Don't give to an ungodly man. Keep back his bread, and don't give it to him, lest he subdue you with it; for you would receive twice as much evil for all the good you would have done to him.

A sinner who refuses to repent is an enemy. Never trust your enemy: "The enemy will speak sweetly with his lips, but in his heart, he will plan to throw you into a pit. The enemy may weep with his eyes, but if he finds an opportunity, he will shed your blood."(12:16)

Chapter 13 teaches us to associate with people of good character otherwise we might adopt bad qualities: "He who touches pitch (tar) will be stained. He who has fellowship with an arrogant man will become like him."(13:1)

Chapter 14 begins by teaching us that true happiness comes when sin is banished from our lives: "Blessed is he whose soul does not condemn him, and who has not given up hope."(14:2) The chapter next teaches us that envy and greed only bring misery. The chapter concludes by teaching us that the pursuit of wisdom brings happiness:

14:20 Blessed is the man who meditates on wisdom, and who reasons by his understanding.

14:21 He who considers her ways in his heart will also have knowledge of her secrets.

Chapter 15 teaches us that if we respect God and his teachings, we will gain wisdom. Sinful people will not gain wisdom. The chapter concludes by telling us that if we sin, don't blame God:

15:11 Don't say, "It is through the Lord that I fell away;" for you shall not do the things that he hates.

15:12 Don't say, "It is he that caused me to err;" for he has no need of a sinful man.

15:13 The Lord hates every abomination; and those who fear him don't love them.

Chapter 16 begins by telling us to not raise "ungodly" children. Next, Sirach tells us that God will show no mercy to sinners and nations that sin will be destroyed. If you are a sinner, you may think that God won't notice you among the multitudes that inhabit the earth, but he does. Accept teaching and gain wisdom: "My son, listen to me, and learn knowledge; pay close attention to my words with your heart."(16:24)

Chapter17 tells us that God created man:

17:3 He clothed them with strength like his own; And made them according to his own image.

17:4 He put the fear of man upon all creatures and gave him dominion over beasts and fowls.

17:6 He gave man a tongue, and eyes, ears, and a mind with which to think.

17:7 He filled them with the knowledge of wisdom; And showed them good and evil.

God created a special covenant with Israel:

17:11 He added to them knowledge and gave them a law of life for a heritage.

17:12 He made an everlasting covenant with them and showed them his judgments.

17:13 Their eyes saw the majesty of his glory and their ears heard the glory of his voice.

17:14 And he said to them, "Beware of all unrighteousness;" And he gave them commandments, each man concerning his neighbor.

Chapter 18 begins by telling us that God created everything, he is the ultimate authority. He shows mercy to everyone, but you must accept his teachings and commandments in order to receive his mercy. The chapter continues to tell us not to spoil our good deeds with harsh words or reproach. If the recipient of a gift or a favor doesn't appreciate your effort, ignore the slight for God will take note of your kindness. Often, a good word is better than a gift. The chapter then offers practical advice: before you speak, learn; before you get sick, take care of your health; before you judge others, examine yourself; humble yourself in good times, don't let success make you arrogant; if you sin, don't wait to repent; prepare yourself before making a vow, do not make a vow you cannot keep; a wise person is always cautious, guarding against wrongdoing. The chapter ends with telling us to protect our souls by practicing self-control:

18:30 Go not after your lusts; And refrain yourself from your appetites.

18:31 If you give fully to your soul the delight of her desire, she will make you the laughing stock of your enemies.

Chapter 19 opens by warning against having a reckless soul which will only lead to death. Be cautious (or wise) in all matters, both small and large. The chapter warns next against gossip:

19:4 He that is hasty to trust is unwise in heart; And he that sins will offend against his own soul.

19:5 He who rejoices in evil will be condemned.

19:6 He who hates gossip will sin less.

19:7 Never repeat what is told you, And you will fare never the worse.

19:8 Whether it be of friend or foe, tell it not; And unless it is a sin to you, reveal it not.

19:9 For he has heard you, and observed you, And when the time comes he will hate you.

19:10 Have you heard a word? let it die with you: Be of good courage, it will not burst you.

Sirach goes on to tell us that being wise and being clever are not the same:

19:20 All wisdom is the fear of the Lord; And in all wisdom is the doing of the law.

19:22 And the knowledge of wickedness is not wisdom; And there is no prudence in the counsel of sinners.

19:23 There is a cleverness and it is an abomination; And there is a fool who merely lacks in wisdom.

19:24 Better is one that has small understanding, and fears God, Than one who has much intelligence and transgresses the law.

Chapter 19 ends with the practical advice that a person is known by their appearance. They are known not only by the clothes they wear but also by their manners, how they talk, how they walk, etc.

Chapter 20 opens by telling us that there are times to speak and times to keep silent:

20:6 There is one that keeps silence, for he has no answer and there is one that keeps silence, knowing it is not his time to speak.

20:7 A wise man will be silent till his time comes; But the braggart and fool will overpass his time.

20:8 He that uses many words will be abhorred; And he that takes to himself authority therein will be hated.

The chapter goes on to compare those who are fools and those who are wise. The gifts and words of fools are worthless because fools lack grace, they are ignorant. In contrast, the words of the wise are prized.

Chapter 21 tells us to avoid sin and gives some advice on how to do so. Don't be arrogant. Listen with an open mind to correction (or criticism), those who don't listen continue on the path to sin. A person who respects God will be able to change their ways. A wise person is known for their wisdom. The truly wise know when they make a mistake and admit it.

Chapter 22 covers several topics. A lazy man is a disgrace. Parents who do not discipline their children are a disgrace. Parents who do not give their children instruction in wisdom are a disgrace. It is impossible to teach a fool anything, they are committed to wasting their lives. Be prudent in your speech, do not let your tongue destroy you.

Chapter 23 opens with a prayer for wisdom. The chapter then discusses how both men and women can be consumed by lust, leading to shame and the destruction of their souls.

Chapter 24 praises wisdom and the benefits she gives to all who seek her. Those who "obey her will not be ashamed, those who work with her will not sin."(24:22)

In Chapter 25, Sirach tells us there are 3 things that make him happy and they are also beautiful in the eyes of the Lord: brothers and sisters who live in harmony; harmony among neighbors; a wife and husband who have a harmonious marriage. There are 3 things kinds of people Sirach hates: a poor man who is arrogant; a rich man who is a liar; an old man who is an adulterer, lacking in understanding. Those who learn wisdom in their youth are made attractive by wisdom in their old age.

Chapter 25 continues with listing 10 things that Sirach considers a blessing: a man who takes joy in his children; a man who sees the fall of his enemies; a man with an understanding wife; a man who does not sin with his tongue; a man who serves those who are worthy; a man who has found prudence; a man who speaks to those who listen; a man who has found wisdom; and, greatest of all, a man who respects God.

Chapter 25 ends with the problems of having an evil wife. He states; "I would rather dwell with a lion and a dragon, than keep house with a wicked woman."(25:16)

Chapter 26 opens by continuing the theme of the importance of having a good wife. Then Sirach list 2 things that grieve him: a soldier who lives in poverty; men of understanding who are held in contempt. Sirach is angered when he sees a righteous man turn to sin. Sirach ends the chapter with a critic of merchants: "A merchant shall hardly keep himself from wrong doing; And a huckster (or peddler) will not be acquitted of sin."(26:29)

Chapter 27 opens with stating that many people sin to make a profit. Riches gained through sin well lead to one's destruction since people are angered by a thief. Sirach next states that you can judge the quality of a man by his ability to reason:

27:5 The furnace will prove the potter's vessels; And the trial of a man is in his reasoning.

27:6 The fruit of a tree declares the husbandry thereof; So is the utterance of the thought of the heart of a man.

27:7 Praise no man before you hear him reason; For this is the trial of men.

Sirach returns to the topic of the importance of speaking wisely, for the talk of fools is "offensive." Sirach ends the chapter by telling us that sinners are punished by their own sins. He who digs a pit for others will fall into it, he who mocks others will be mocked, those who wish pain upon the innocent will be consumed by pain, and so on. The last verse states: "Wrath and anger, these also are abominations; And a sinful man will possess them."(27:30)

Chapter 28 opens by telling us to never seek revenge. Instead: "Forgive your neighbor the hurt that he has done you; And then your sins will be pardoned when you pray."(28:2) Sirach goes on to tell us to stop quarrelling and spreading evil talk. Never be hot-tempered and try to abstain from strife. Never slander anyone: "Curse the slanderous and deceitful: For he has destroyed many that were at peace."(28:13)

Chapter 29 tells us to help our neighbor. If a neighbor needs a loan, give them the loan. If you receive a loan, do not be slow in paying it back. A loan is not a sudden windfall, do not put off paying it back. If you do not plan to pay a loan back, do not ask for it. Not paying a loan back in a timely manner is the same as stealing. If a neighbor is in great need, do not hesitate to help them with alms or charity. Do not turn away those in true need, do not send them away empty handed.

Chapter 30 tells us that parents who love their children discipline them and avoid spoiling them. Good health is important. A cheerful heart is also important:

30:21 Do not give your soul over to sorrow; do not distress yourself in your own counsel.

30:22 Gladness of heart is the life of a man; And the joyfulness of a man lengthens his days.

30:23 Love your own soul and comfort your heart: And remove sorrow far from you; For sorrow has destroyed many, And there is no profit therein.

Chapter 31 tells us not to let concern over money destroy your sleep. Those who love gold and profit will be consumed by the pursuit of riches. Blessed is the rich person who does not chase after gold and wealth. Such a person tends to be generous and reinforces good in the community. The chapter ends by advising us to eat in moderation, do not be a glutton at the table. A small amount of food is sufficient and moderate eating will lead to sound sleep and good health. Do not get drunk. People say and do bad things when drunk.

Chapter 32 tells us that if we host a dinner, be polite and thoughtful to the guest. Seat yourself last. Speak only when necessary, listen to your guest. A good host is humble.

Chapter 33 tells us that only fools and hypocrites pretend to respect God. God will rescue his true followers from evil. Try not to give others power over you. If you have responsibility for servants (or slaves), treat them with respect and use good judgment in dealing with them. There needs to be discipline in the work place as well as at home.

In chapter 34, Sirach warns us that dreams can be false. Do not allow lies and false dreams to destroy your life. God alone will lead you down the right path. Travel can be useful in increasing one's understanding of the world. God blesses those who follow him with courage and support. God hates offerings (or alms) from the ungodly. God does not want gifts from people who have come by their wealth dishonestly.

In contrast, chapter 35 tells us the God is eager to accept the offerings of the righteous. Charity from honest people is always looked upon by God with grace. God cares about true justice and mercy. He knows what is in your heart, he cannot be bribed.

In chapter 36, Sirach prays for Israel, asking God to show mercy to his chosen people. Sirach ends the chapter by telling us that we each need to use are own discernment (based on God's guidance and teachings) to distinguish the truth from lies. We must think for ourselves.

Chapter 37 carries on the theme of the importance of discernment. Use good judgment in choosing your friends, know their character. Use good judgment in choosing your counselors. Know their true motives. Do not seek advice from those who are envious or hate you. Seek the advice of Godly people.

Chapter 38 opens by telling us to honor physicians. Do not ignore the advice and medicines that physicians offer. Good health is precious, don't throw it away. When death does come to a loved one, mourn for as many days as you need. Allow others to help you get through the despair. But do not allow grief to overcome you, Grief can destroy you. Do not "give your heart over to grief."

Chapter 39 opens with Sirach praising students of wisdom. He then concludes the chapter by praising God's works.

Sirach opens chapter 40 with a discussion of life's hardships. We all share in these hardships:

40:3 From one that sits on a throne of glory, to one who is humbled in earth and ashes;

40:4 From one that wears purple and a crown, to one clothed in burlap.

40:5 There is anger, jealousy, trouble, and unrest; And fear of death, and fury, and strife;

But the wise will in the end triumph, while the unwise will perish:

40:12 All bribery and injustice shall be blotted out, good faith shall stand forever.

40:13 The wealth of the unjust shall be dried up like a river, and crash like thunder in a storm.

40:14 A generous person will rejoice; evil doers will come to ruin.

Sirach returns to a discussion of death in chapter 41. We should not be afraid of death since all living things die. The good that a virtuous person does survives their death. Sirach then concludes the chapter on the importance of shame. It is important to feel shame for inappropriate actions so we will not repeat them. He lists some of these inappropriate actions such as stealing, poor table manners, lust, rejecting a relative, giving a gift in bad faith and gossip.

Chapter 42 opens with Sirach listing some things that we should never be ashamed of such as not committing a sin, respecting God and his law, honest business dealings and the profits (or losses) from these dealings, giving justice to the ungodly, correcting the foolish or stupid or those guilty of sexual immorality, and protecting yourself from thieves and evil doers. Sirach then tells us that fathers must always protect the virtue and character of their daughters. He then ends the chapter by once again praising God and his works.

In chapter 43, Sirach praises the beauty of God's creation, both in the sky and on the earth.

In chapters 44-50, Sirach praises the heroes of Israel's past. These include Enoch, Noah, Abraham, Aaron, Phineas, all the Judges, David, Solomon, Elijah and many others. He ends chapter 50 first with an odd statement about his dislike for the Philistines, the people of Shechem, and the Samaritans. Then Sirach identifies himself as the author of the book: "I have written in this book instructions for understanding and knowledge. I Jesus, the son of Sirach Eleazar, of Jerusalem, who out of his heart poured forth wisdom."(50:27)

Sirach opens chapter 51 with a prayer or psalm giving thanks to God. He then talks about the joy he gained by pursuing wisdom and studying the Word of God. Sirach ends the book with the following:

51:29 May your soul rejoice in His mercy, and may you not be put to shame in praising Him.

51:30 Do your work before the appointed time comes, and in His time, God will give you your reward.

FRANCIS BROWN

9. Studying the Bible

People often ask why study the Bible? It is difficult to understand, it is ancient, and why would it apply to modern society? Scripture has always been difficult to understand, even when it was new. As we know from Sirach's grandson, translating ancient Hebrew has always been hard, even in ancient times. The grandson and the author of the Wisdom of Solomon both lived in what was then the "modern" Hellenistic world. This was a world of exciting new ideas but also a pagan world filled with pagan gods. Both authors thought their "modern world" lacked wisdom. Sirach's grandson felt that people needed his grandfather's common-sense approach to wisdom. The author of the Wisdom of Solomon wanted to remind people that the new gods were no more powerful than the gods of Egypt a thousand years earlier. Both authors believed that there will always be new ideas, but true wisdom is timeless and should not be abandoned. The success of both works proved they were right. Now, a little over a thousand years later, we live in a modern secular world filled with competing ideas and philosophies. Is the need for wisdom any less now than it was in ancient Alexandria?

Too often, people treat reading the Bible as a kind of homework assignment. They worry about what everything means and are overwhelmed by it all. Scripture is not there to burden us, it is there to help us. We all need to follow Sirach's example and make studying Scripture a source of joy. A good place to start is by picking a reading Bible. There are many Bible translations in different formats to choose from, and you may have to go through several before finding the one that's right for you. But once you pick a reading Bible, read it. Don't worry about what a word means or who a person is, just read. You can study later. When you do this, you will find that you understand more than you thought possible. The Bible helps us to understand by repeating major points. If you don't get the meaning in one verse, you will get it in another verse. The more often you read Scripture, the more you will understand. Your reading Bible will become like an old friend, giving advice and support when you need it. It is best, though, not to depend solely on one translation of the Bible. You should have a few different Bible translations (and study Bibles) in your library since every translation has its strengths and weaknesses.

When you read the Bible, you join millions of others around the world in a common pursuit of wisdom. You also join Sirach, Jerome, and all those in the past who studied Scripture and sought wisdom, from ancient times on. Scripture is a gift, a gift that benefits anyone who accepts it.

.

Printed in Great Britain
by Amazon